FROM HISTORIAN TO DISSIDENT:
THE BOOK OF JOHN WHITMER

FROM HISTORIAN TO DISSIDENT: THE BOOK OF JOHN WHITMER

EDITED BY BRUCE N. WESTERGREN

Signature Books • Salt Lake City • 1995

To my parents, Murry and Mary Westergren,
and
To our kids, Ginger, Nermal, George, Friday,
Mama Cat, Birdie, Smokie, Chino, and Sherlock,
and
To Elder Michael Carlson, to whom I owe
a great many steak dinners.

JACKET DESIGN BY RON STUCKI
JACKET ILLUSTRATION BY CAROL NORBY

❖

∞ *From Historian to Dissident* was printed on acid-free paper
and was composed, printed, and bound in the United States.

❖

© 1995 Signature Books in association with Smith Research Associates.
All rights reserved. Signature Books is a trademark of Signature Books, Inc.

99　98　97　96　95　　6　5　4　3　2　1

❖

Library of Congress Cataloging-in-Publication Data
Whitmer, John, 1802-1878.
From historian to dissident : the book of John Whitmer /
edited by Bruce Westergren.
p.　cm.
Includes bibliographical references and index.
ISBN 1-56085-043-4
1. Church of Jesus Christ of Latter-Day Saints —History—19th century.
2. Mormon Church—History—19th century.
3. Whitmer, John, 1802-1878.　I. Westergren, Bruce.　II. Title.
BX8611.W535　1995
289.3'09'034—dc20　　　　　　94-46821
CIP

CONTENTS

Editor's Introduction VII
Abbreviations to Frequently Cited Sources . . . XV

Chapter 1. Preparing the Way 3
Chapter 2. A Paid Ministry 27
Chapter 3. Competing Prophets 37
Chapter 4. Welcoming Unbelievers 47
Chapter 5. Gathering to Ohio 51
Chapter 6. Becoming Scribe 55
Chapter 7. The High Priesthood 69
Chapter 8. A Change of Venue 81
Chapter 9. The Land of Zion 85
Chapter 10. Eviction 101
Chapter 11. "Your Humble Petitioners" . . 111
Chapter 12. The Court of Public Sentiment 125

CHAPTER 13.	THE ARMIES OF ISRAEL	131
CHAPTER 14.	RETREAT TO KIRTLAND	135
CHAPTER 15.	TWELVE APOSTLES	139
CHAPTER 16.	MUMMIES AND MURMURINGS	165
CHAPTER 17.	ANOINTINGS	173
CHAPTER 18.	THE HOUSE OF THE LORD	177
CHAPTER 19.	EXCOMMUNICATION	179
CHAPTER 20.	WAR AND BLOODSHED	183
CHAPTER 21.	NAUVOO	191
CHAPTER 22.	DISPERSION	199

Index 203

EDITOR'S INTRODUCTION

John Whitmer was born on August 27, 1802, in Pennsylvania. He was baptized for the remission of sins by Oliver Cowdery in June 1829 at the age of twenty-six, one year before the organization of the Church of Christ (later Church of Jesus Christ of Latter-day Saints). He was later ordained an elder on June 9, 1830, and a high priest on June 3, 1831. On February 10, 1833, he married Sarah Jackson in Jackson County, Missouri.

Much of Whitmer's career in Mormonism was spent in recording its history and publishing its doctrine. He acted as a scribe during part of the translation of the Book of Mormon and also during the new translation of the Bible. Under direction of Joseph Smith he copied a number of revelations and prepared them for publication in what would eventually become the Book of Commandments. He left Ohio in company with Oliver Cowdery in November 1831 to take the Book of Commandments manuscript to Missouri, arriving on January 5, 1832.

Whitmer was officially called as church historian on March 8, 1831, and on June 12 he began keeping his narrative history, "The Book of John Whitmer, kept by commandment." Upon returning to Kirtland, Ohio, in May 1835 to participate in the dedication of the temple, he was asked to remain in Kirtland

and serve as editor of the *Latter Day Saints' Messenger and Advocate*. This assignment lasted until March 1836, and by July Whitmer was back in Missouri.

Perhaps best remembered as one of the eight witnesses of the Book of Mormon, Whitmer and seven other people had gone with Joseph Smith into the woods near the Smith family farm in Manchester Township, New York, in June 1829 where Smith had allowed all to see and handle the gold plates from which he had dictated the Book of Mormon. Whitmer joined with the rest in signing a written testimony of their experience, which has been published in every edition of the Book of Mormon since.[1]

Whitmer figured prominently in the leadership of the church in Missouri as well. At the time of vigilante action against the Saints in Jackson County, he served on the committee which negotiated a final settlement with residents allowing Mormons to leave peacefully—an agreement later violated by agitators. Moving to Clay County, he sent several petitions for redress of his losses to Governor Daniel Dunklin and handled a great deal of business as an agent for the church. On July 8, 1834, Whitmer was ordained a member of the presidency of the church in Missouri and served as a counselor to his brother David.

On April 7, 1837, Whitmer was appointed to serve on a committee responsible for the purchase and sale of town lots in Clay County, Missouri. Lands had been purchased in May 1836, but the increasing number of Mormon immigrants moving into the region made the acquisition of additional land imperative. Using church money, John Whitmer and W. W. Phelps purchased the site for the town of Far West, entering land in their names and, instead of turning over the full proceeds from the sale of lots to the church, apparently kept a commission for themselves. Bitter feelings developed, and in November 1837 John Whitmer and the rest of the Missouri presidency were publicly questioned in a church conference. Explanations were made, and the congregation was satisfied. However, in January and February 1838 it was discovered that the presidency had sold their own property in Jackson County, in essence capitulating to the vigilantes. At the time such an act was considered tantamount to denying the faith. In addition, all three faced charges of violating the Word of Wisdom by periodically drinking tea and coffee. After considering the evidence, church members rejected the entire presidency. On March 10, 1838, all three men were excommunicated from the church.

John Whitmer remained in Missouri after the Mormons were later driven out of the state by state militia. Whitmer farmed and raised livestock. He never rejoined the church, nor did he ever retract his testimony of the Book of Mormon or Joseph Smith. He died at Far West on July 11, 1878.[2]

Whitmer's history is a continuation of an account kept by Oliver Cowdery which began with the discovery of the Book of Mormon plates and ended on June 12, 1831. Cowdery's record is not extant; its material, however, was probably used in creating the *Messenger and Advocate* account which covered the years 1823-27. Whitmer's narrative provides a detailed picture of events in New York prior to the move to Ohio, including the reasons for that move; the text of a number of Joseph Smith's revelations, primarily those found in the Doctrine and Covenants; and an account of the Missouri troubles, with copies of petitions and correspondence between Mormon leaders and state and federal officials.

Whitmer's first-hand account ends with his excommunication in March 1838, which he duly recorded in chapter 19, followed by a prayer for eventual forgiveness and a farewell. This is continued in chapter 20, written at least a year later, which is a bitter recital of persecution of his family and those of other Mormon dissenters by former fellow believers. After Whitmer's excommunication, he and other dissenters continued to live peaceably among the Latter-day Saints—until Sidney Rigdon delivered his famous June 19, 1838, "Salt Sermon." Although no copy of the speech exists in its entirety, from various journal accounts it appears that Rigdon declared open war on any and all dissenters.[3] According to Whitmer's record, it was shortly after this time that he, Oliver Cowdery, David Whitmer, W. W. Phelps, and others, along with their families, were forced to flee Far West for the town of Richmond in Clay County. John Whitmer blamed the Danites—or "Gideonites," as he referred to them—for the formers' flight, and he ultimately held Smith and Rigdon responsible for what he saw as a new, rigid structure of church discipline, completely contrary to the spirit of the restored Mormon gospel.

Through information from friends still among the Mormons, Whitmer stayed in touch with events following the church's expulsion from Missouri in 1839. He recorded in his manuscript the rise of Nauvoo, Illinois, and the 1844 murder of Joseph Smith and his brother Hyrum at the hands of the mob in Carthage. He blamed the church's problems in Missouri and Illinois on polygamy, the continued operations of the Danite band, Joseph's "pride" and "lust after the forbidden things of God," and the Saints' "vile behavior" toward non-Mormons.

Whitmer also discussed the rivalry for leadership of the church after Joseph Smith's death, sympathizing, at least initially, with James J. Strang. There is no evidence, however, that Whitmer ever formerly allied himself with that group.

This manuscript is apparently a later draft; the whereabouts of the original is not known. There are several things which indicate that this volume is not the original. First, the last sentence is incomplete and the remaining pages are blank. Second, on page 22 of this draft Whitmer first records the date of a church conference as taking place on June 4, 1831, then afterwards inserts the word "March" in the space above it. Finally, on page 28, when listing some of the names of those ordained to various priesthood offices during an 1831 church conference, Whitmer lists the names of some who later left the church, specifically Ezra Booth, Harvey Whitlock, and Joseph Wakefield. These men did not leave the church until 1833. In the same entry he lists his own name among those who fell from the faith, although he was not excommunicated until 1838. He also lists the names of Joseph Smith, Jr., and Joseph Smith, Sr., which shows his feelings that Joseph Smith, Jr., had become a fallen prophet—feelings he did not entertain until 1838.

The manuscript ends at the bottom of page 96 with the succession of Brigham Young and the Twelve to the presidency of the LDS church. The last sentence is incomplete. Whitmer's original manuscript is a book of ordinary ledger-size paper approximately 300 pages long. Ninety-six of the pages were written on. Thus, although it may seem unusual for the last sentence in the record to end in the middle, apparently that was all Whitmer wrote.[4]

PROVENANCE

The original manuscript remained in John Whitmer's possession until his death in 1878. It then came into the possession of one of his nieces, a daughter of David Whitmer, and her husband, George Schweich. After two previous attempts, in

1893 Assistant LDS Church Historian Andrew Jenson was finally allowed to see the original manuscript and make a handwritten copy of it to take back to Salt Lake City with him. Schweich, a non-Mormon, helped Jenson proofread his copy against the original manuscript. Once back in Salt Lake City Jenson made a typewritten copy of his handwritten duplicate. After several more close comparisons, Jenson placed a copy on file in the LDS Church Historian's Office and sent a second copy to the Reorganized Church of Jesus Christ of Latter Day Saints in Independence, Missouri.[5]

Whitmer's history has previously appeared in print three times. In 1908 the RLDS church published it in its periodical, *Journal of History*; in 1966 a version edited by Jerald and Sandra Tanner was published by Modern Microfilm in Salt Lake City; and in 1980 Herald House published a new version edited by F. Mark McKiernan and Roger D. Launius.[6] This third edition differs in places from the Jenson typescript and the original document.

"The Book of John Whitmer" is reproduced here by permission of the Library and Archives of the Reorganized Church of Jesus Christ of Latter Day Saints headquartered in Independence, Missouri. Special thanks to Steve Sorensen, director of LDS church archives in Salt Lake City, and to Ron Romig, church archivist for the RLDS church, for the material they shared. They saved me from several egregious blunders.

EDITORIAL STYLE

The following conventions have been adopted for this book. Chapter titles are my creation, not Whitmer's. Spelling, punctuation, and capitalization have been retained as they appear in the original. Where the source was unclear, current usage has been substituted. Insertions placed above the line with a caret (^) have been placed between angle brackets on the line at the point of insertion: <the blessing given>.

Characters and words stricken out in the original have been retained. Missing or illegible characters or words are indicated by dots and dashes within square brackets, dots [..] representing the approximate number of missing letters and dashes [— —] the approximate number of missing words.

Editorial insertions that enlarge the original text or supply missing or illegible words are enclosed in square brackets: W[illia]m. Editorial comments not part of the text are enclosed in square brackets and italicized [*page ends*]. Underlined words are italicized; if the source was a published pamphlet, italics are used.

Bracketed page numbers designate the beginning of each new page: [p. 15]. The beginning of unnumbered pages are shown by parentheses within square brackets: [(p. 11)].

Superscripted letters are lowered: Jr to Jr.

Paragraph indentations are, for the most part, modern and done for the convenience of the reader. Annotations have been supplied where needed.

NOTES

1. See Anderson, *Witnesses*, 123-34.

2. *LDSBE*, 1:251-52; Cook, *Revelations*, 25-26. Cook claims that beginning in 1836-37 Whitmer and W. W. Phelps started "to administer affairs of the Church in Missouri independent[ly] of [the] high council." However, the minutes of the meetings in which Whitmer was appointed to purchase and sell land and the subsequent disciplinary hearings indicate that the surveys and purchases were carried out in accordance with his instructions. Whitmer and Phelps were charged with skim-

ming the profits for compensation and for selling their personal land in Jackson County. See *Far West Record,* 103-106, 121-27, 135-41, 145-50.

3. See Stephen C. LeSueur, *The 1838 Mormon War in Missouri* (Columbia: University of Missouri Press, 1987), 37-40.

4. Andrew Jenson to Franklin D. Richards, 5 Sept. 1893, archives, Historical Department, Church of Jesus Christ of Latter-day Saints, Salt Lake City, Utah.

5. "Andrew Jenson and the History of John Whitmer," typescript, LDS archives. A comparison of Jenson's typescript with Whitmer's original manuscript shows no significant variations.

6. F. Mark McKiernan and Roger Launius, eds., *An Early Latter Day Saint History: The Book of John Whitmer* (Independence, MO: Herald Publishing House, 1980).

ABBREVIATIONS TO FREQUENTLY CITED SOURCES

Anderson, *Witnesses*: Richard L. Anderson, *Investigating the Book of Mormon Witnesses* (Salt Lake City: Deseret Book Co., 1981).

Backman, *Heavens*: Milton V. Backman, Jr., *The Heavens Resound: A History of the Latter-day Saints in Ohio, 1830-1838* (Salt Lake City: Deseret Book Co., 1983).

Cook, *Revelations*: Lyndon W. Cook, *The Revelations of the Prophet Joseph Smith* (Provo, UT: Seventy's Mission Bookstore, 1981).

D&C: *Doctrine and Covenants of the Church of Jesus Christ of Latter-day Saints* (Salt Lake City: Church of Jesus Christ of Latter-day Saints, 1981), section and verse numbers.

Far West Record: Donald Q. Cannon and Lyndon W. Cook, eds., *Far West Record: Minutes of The Church of Jesus Christ of Latter-day Saints, 1830-1841* (Salt Lake City: Deseret Book Co., 1983).

HC:	Joseph Smith et al., *History of the Church of Jesus Christ of Latter-day Saints*, ed. B. H. Roberts, 7 vols. 2d rev. ed. (Salt Lake City: Deseret Book Co., 1978).
LDSBE:	Andrew Jenson, *LDS Biographical Encyclopedia*, 4 vols. (Salt Lake City: Andrew Jenson History Co., 1901; reprint ed., Salt Lake City: Western Epics, 1971).
Pratt, *Autobiography*:	Parley P. Pratt, *Autobiography of Parley P. Pratt*, ed. Parley P. Pratt, Jr. (Salt Lake City: Deseret Book Co., 1985).
Wood:	Wilford C. Wood, *Joseph Smith Begins His Work*, 2 vols. (Salt Lake City: Wilford C. Wood, 1958, 1962). Wood's two volumes contain photolithographic reproductions of the 1830 Book of Mormon, the 1833 Book of Commandments, and the 1835 Kirtland edition of the Doctrine and Covenants and Lectures on Faith. Since this work is an exact reproduction, pagination is the same as the original publication. Consequently, to avoid confusion, when the 1833 Book of Commandments text is referred to, it is cited as Wood, 2[1833]:, followed by page numbers. The 1835 Doctrine and Covenants text is cited as Wood, 2[1835]:, followed by page numbers.

The Book of John Whitmer
[Kept by Comndt.]

Chapter I

Preparing the Way

[(p. 1)] I shall proceed to continue this record, being commanded of the Lord and Savior Jesus Christ, to write the things that transpire in this church, (inasmuch as they come to my knowledge,) in these last days. It is now June the twelfth one thousand eight hundred and thirty one years since the coming of our Lord and Savior, in the flesh.

Not many days after my brethren, Oliver Cowdery,[1] Peter Whitmer, Jr.[2] Parley P. Pratt,[3] and Ziba Peterson[4]: Received a commandment of the Lord, through Joseph Smith Jr.,[5] to take their journey to the Lamanites, and preach the gospel of our Lord and Savior, among them, and establish the church of Christ among them. They journeyed as far West as the State of Ohio; and through the divine influences of the Holy Spirit, by the assistance of the Lord, they built a branch of the church, in Geauga Co. State of Ohio, which consisted of about one hundred and thirty members.[6]

And now it came to pass, that before they proceeded, on their journey from this place [Geauga County], There was a man whose name was sidney Rigdon,[7] he having been an instrument in the hands of the Lord of doing much good. He was in search of truth, consequently he received the fulness of the gospel with gladness of heart, even the book of Mormon; it being what he was in search after, notwithstanding it was some days before he obtained a witness from the Lord, of the truth of his work. After several days the Lord heard his cries, and answered his prayers, and by vision showed to him, that this eminated from him [God] and must remain, it being the Fulness of the gospel of Jesus Christ, first unto the Gentiles and then unto the Jews.

Now it came to pass, after sidney Rigdon, ~~and~~ <was> received into this church, that he was ordained an Elder, under the hands of Oliver Cowdery. He having much anxiety to see Joseph Smith Jr. the seer whom the Lord had raised up in these last days. Therefore he took his Journey to the State of New York where Joseph Resided.

There was another man whose name is Edward Partridge,[8] [p. 2] who was also desirous, to see the Seer, Therefore, he accompanied Sidney, and journeyed with him, to behold this man of God even Joseph Smith Jr. he being desirous to know the truth of these things: But not having confidence enough to inquire at the hand of God, Therefore he sought testimony of man, and he obtained it, and received the truth and obeyed the divine requirements, and was also ordained an Elder unto this church, to preach repentance and remission of Sins, unto this idolertrous generation.

Therefore, after Sidney Rigdon had been at Palmyra a few days he proclaimed the gospel, in those regions rount about, at which the people stood trembling and amased, so powerful were his words, and some obeyed, the gospel, and came forth out of the water, rejoicing with Joy which is <unspeakable and> full of glory. From thence he journeyed to Fayette, where Joseph lived, and there he also proclaimed the gospel, ~~and~~ in the regions round about <and> there were numbers added.

Now in these days Sidney Rigdon was desirous to have the Seer enquire of the Lord, to know what the will of the Lord was concerning him. Accordingly Joseph enquired of the Lord, and these are the words that were spoken to him, saying[9]: Listen to the Lord your God, even Alpha and Omega, the beginning and the end, whose course is one eternal round, the same to day as yesterday and for ever. I am Jesus Christ, the Son of God, who was crucified for the sins of the world, even as many as will believe in my name, that they may become the sons of God, even one in me as I am in the Father, as the Father is one in me, that we may be one.

Behold, verily, verily, I say unto my servant Sidney Rigdon, I have looked upon thee and thy works, I have heard thy prayers and prepared thee for a greater work. Thou art blessed, for thou shalt do great things. Behold thou wast sent forth even as John, to prepare the way before me, and before Elijah which should come, and thou knew it not. Thou didst baptize by water unto repentance, but they received not the holy Ghost; but now I give unto you a commandment, that thou shalt baptize by water, [(p. 3)] and they shall receive the Holy Ghost, by the laying on of the hands, even as the apostles of old.

And it shall come to pass, that there shall be a great work in the land even among the Gentiles, for their folly and obaminati[ons] shall be made manifest, in the eyes of all people: for I am God and mine arm is not shortened and I will show miracles, signs and wonders, unto all those who believe in my name. And whoso shall ask it in my name, in faith, they shall cast out devils; they shall heal the sick; they shall cause the blind to receive their sight, and the deaf to hear, and the dumb to speak, and the lame to walk: and the time Speedily cometh that great things shall be shown unto the children of men: but without faith shall not any thing be shown forth, except desolation upon Babylon, the same which has made all nations drink of the wine of the wrath of her fornication. And there are non[e] that doeth good except those who are ready to receive the fulness of the gospel, which I have sent forth to this generation.

Wherefore, I have called upon the weak things of the world, those who are unlearned and despised, to thresh the nations by the power of my Spirit: and their arm shall be my arm, and I will be their shield and their buckler, and I will gird up their loins, and they shall fight manfulley for me: and their enemies shall be under their feet; and I will let fall the sword in their behalf; and by the fire of mine indignation will I preserve them. And the poor and the meek shall have the gosple preached unto them, and they shall be looking forth for the time of my coming, for it is nigh at hand: and they shall learn the parable of the fig tree: for even now already summer is nigh, and I have sent forth the fulness of my gospel by the hand of my servant Joseph: and in weakness have I blessed him, and I have given unto him the Keys of the mysteries of these things which have been sealed, even things which were from the foundation of the world, and the things which shall come from this time until the time of my coming, if he abide in me, and if not, another will I plant in his stead.

[p. 4] Wherefore, watch over him that his faith fail not, and it shall be given by the Comforter, the Holy Ghost, that knoweth all things: and a commandment I give unto thee, that thou shalt write for him: and the scriptures shall be given <even> as they are in mine own bosom, to the salvation of mine own elect: for they will hear my voice, and shall see me, and shall not be asleep, and shall abide the day of my coming, for they shall be purified even as I am pure. And now I say unto you, tarry with him and he shall journey with you: forsake him not and surely these things shall be fulfilled. And inasmuch as ye do not write, behold it shall be given unto him to prophesy: and thou shalt preach my gospel, and call on the holy prophets, to prove his words, as they shall be given him.

Keep all the commandments and covenants by which you are bound, and I will cause the heavens to shake for your good: and Satan shall tremble; and Zion shall rejoice upon the hills, and flourish; and Israel shall be saved in my own due time. And by the keys by which <I> have ~~have~~ given, shall they be led and no more be confounded at all. Lift up your hearts and be glad: your redemption draweth nigh. Fear not little flock, the kingdom is yours until I come. Behold I come quickle, even so: Amen.

Now, after the Lord had made known, what he wanted that his servant Sidney should do, he went to writing the things which the Lord showed unto his servant the Seer. The Lord made known, some of the hidden things of ~~the~~ kingdom ~~of God~~; for he unfolded the prophesy of Enoch the sevanth from Adam.[10] After they had written this prophecy, the Lord spake to them again, and gave further directions.[11] Behold I say unto you, that it is not expedient in me that ye should translate any more until ye shall go to the Ohio; and this because of the enemy and for your sakes. And again, I say unto you, that ye shall not go until ye have preached ~~the~~ <my> gospel in these parts, and have strengthened up the church, whithersoever it is found, and more especially in Colesville for behold they pray unto [p. 5] me in much faith.

And again, a commandment I give unto the church, that it is expedient in me that they should assemble together at the Ohio, against the time that my Servant Oliver Cowdery shall return unto them. Behold here is wisdom, and let every man choose for himself until I come; even so: Amen.

After the above directions were received, Joseph and Sidney went to the several churches preaching and propheceing wherever they went, and greatly strengthened the churches that were built unto the Lord. Joseph prophesied saying: God is about to destroy this generation, and Christ will descend from heaven in power and great glory, with all the holy angels with him to take vengeance upon the wicked and they that know not God: Sidney preached the gospel and proved his words from the holy prophets; and so powerful were their words, that the people who heard them speak were amased, and trembled, and knew not whereunto this thing would grow. The adversary of all righteousness being crafty, and beguiled the people, and stirred them up to anger, against the words spoken, and has blinded their eyes and is leading them down to darkness, ~~and~~ misery and wo! This generation abounds in ignorance, superstition, selfishness, idoletry, and priestcraft, for this generation is truly led by priests, even hireling priests whose god is the substance of this worlds goods which waxeth old and is begining to fade away who look for their hire every one from his quarter.

Because of the abominations that are abroad in the world, it is hard for those who receive the fulness of the gospel, and came into the new and everlasting covenant <to> get clear of the traditions of their forefathers: and are [slow] to be made to believe the commandments that came forth in these last days for the upbuilding of the kingdom of God, and the salvation of those who believe.

The time had now come for the general conference to be held [in Fayette, New York]. Which was the first of January 1831.[12] <and> according to this appointment the saints assembled themselves together. After [p. 6] transacting the necessary business, Joseph the seer addressed the congregation, and exhorted them to stand fast; looking forward considering the end of their salvation. The solemnities of eternity rested on the congregation, and having previously received a revelation to go to Ohio,[13] they desired to know somewhat more concerning this matter. Therefor, the Seer enquired of the Lord in the presence of the whole congregation, and thus came the word of the Lord saying[14]:

Thus saith the Lord God, even Jesus Christ the great I AM, Alpha and Omega, the beginning and the end. The same which looked upon the wide expance of eternity, and all the seraphic host of heaven, before the world was made; the same which knoweth all things, for all things are present before mine eyes. I am the same which spake and the world was made, and all things came by me: I am the same which have taken the Zion of Enoch into mine own bosom, and verily I say, even as many as have believed on my name, for I am Christ, and in my own name by virtue the of the blood which I have spilt, have I plead before the Father for them; But behold the residue of the wicked have I kept in chains of darkness, until the judgment of the great day, which shall come at the end of the earth, and even so will I cause the wicked to be kept, that will not hear my voice but harden their hearts, and wo, wo, wo is their doom.

Behold, verily, verily I say unto you, that mine eyes are upon you; I am in your midst and ye cannot see me, but the day cometh that ye shall see me and know that I am: for the veil of darkness shall soon be rent, and he that is not purified shall not abide the day: Wherefore, gird up your loins and be prepared. Behold the kingdom is yours, and ~~ye~~ <enemy> shall not overcome.

Verily I say unto you, ye are clean but not all, and there is none else with whom I am well pleased, for all flesh is corruptable before me, and the powers of darkness prevail [p. 7] upon the earth, among the children of men, in the presence of all the hosts of heaven, which causes silence to reign, and all eternity is pained; and the angels are waiting the great command to reap down the earth, to gather the tares that they may be burned: and behold the enemy is combined.

And now I show unto you a mystery, a thing which is had in secret chambers, to bring to pass even your destruction, in process of time, and ye knew it not, but now I tell it unto you, not because of your iniquity, neither your hearts of unbelief, for verily some of you are guilty before me; but I will be merciful unto your weakness. Therefore be ye strong from henceforth; fear not for the kingdom is yours: and for your salvation I give unto you a commandment, for I have heard your prayers, and the poor have complained before me, and the rich have I made, and all flesh is mine, and I am no respector of persons. And I have made the earth rich, and behold ~~I have made the earth rich~~ it is my footstool: wherefore, again I will stand upon it: and I hold forth and deign to give unto you greater riches, even a land of promise; a land flowing with milk and honey, upon which there shall be no curse when the Lord cometh: and I will give it unto you for the land of your inheritance, if you seek it with all your hearts: and this shall be my covenant with you, ye shall have it for the land of your inheritance, and for the inheritance of your children for ever, while the earth shall stand, and ye shall possess it again in eternity no more to pass away.[15]

But verily I say unto you, that in time ye shall have no King nor ruler, for I will be your King and watch over you—Wherefore, hear my voice and follow me, and ye shall be a free people, and ye shall have no laws but my laws, when I come, for I am your Lawgiver, and what can stay my hand? But verily I say unto you, teach one another according to the office wherewith I have appointed you, and let every man esteem his brother as himself, and practice virtue and holyness before me. And again I say unto you, let every man esteem his brother as himself; for [p. 8] what man among you having twelve sons, and is no respector to them, and they serve him obediently, and he saith unto the one, be thou clothed in robes and sit thou here; and to the other, be thou clothed in raggs and sit thou there, and looketh upon his sons and saith I am just.

Behold, this I have given unto you as a parable, and it is even as I am: I say unto you, be one; and if ye are not one, ye are not mine. And again I say unto you, that the enemy in the secret chamber seeketh your lives; Ye hear of wars in far countries, and you say there will soon be great wars in far countries, but ye know not the hearts of them in your own land: I tell you these things because of your prayers: Wherefore treasure up wisdom in your bosoms, lest the wickedness of men reveal these things unto you, by their wickedness in a manner which ~~will~~ <shall> speak in your ears, with a voice louder than that which shall shake [the] earth: but if ye are prepared ye shall not fear.

And that you might escape the power of the enemy, and be gathered unto me a righteous people, without spot and blameless: wherefore for this cause I gave unto you the commandment that ye should go to the Ohio: and there I will give unto you my law; and there you shall be endowed with power from on high, and from thence, whomsoever I will shall go forth among all nations, and it shall be told them what they shall do: for I have a great work laid up in store: for Israel shall be saved, and I will lead them whithersoever I will, and no power shall stay my hand.

And now I give unto the church in these parts, a commandment, that certain men among them shall be appointed, and they shall be appointed by the voice of the church, and they shall look to the poor and administer to their releaf, that they shall not suffer; and send them forth to the place which I have commanded them, and this shall be their work, to govern the affairs of the property of this church. And they [p. 9] that have farms that cannot be sold, let them be left or rented, as seemeth them good. See that all things are preserved, and when men are endowed with power from on high, and sent forth, all these things shall be gathered unto the bosom of the church.

And if ye seek the riches which it is the will of the Father to give unto you, ye shall be the richest of all people; for ye shall have the riches of eternity; and it must needs be that the riches of the earth is mine to give; but beware of pride, lest ye become as the Nephites of old. And again I say unto you, I give unto you a commandment, that Elder, Priest, Teacher, and ~~people~~, also member, go to with his might, with the labor of his hands, to prepare and accomplish the things which I have commanded. And let your preaching be the warning voice, every one to his neighbor, in mildness and in meekness. And go ye out from among the wicked. Save yourselves. Be ye clean that bear the vessels of the Lord; even so: Amen.

After the Lord had manifested the above words, through Joseph the Seer, there were some divisions among the congregation, some would not receive the above as the word of the Lord: but [held] that Joseph had invented it himself to deceive the people that in the end he might get gain. Now this was because, their hearts were not right in the sight of the Lord, for they wanted to serve God and man; but our Savior has declared that it was impossible to do so.

The conference was now closed, and the Lord had manifested his will to his people. Therefore they made preperations to Journey to the Ohio, with their wives, and children and all that they possessed, to obey the commandment of the Lord. After these things were done Joseph and Sidney went to Colesville[16] to do the will of the Lord in that part of the land and to strengthen the disciples in that part of the vineyard, and preach the gosple to a hardened and a wicked people, and it is fearful that they are all delivered over to the hardness of heart and blindness, [p. 10] so that they cannot be brought to repentance. For when Sidney and the Revelator arrivd there, they held prayer meetings, among the disciples, and they also held public meetings but it was all in vain, they threatend to kill them. Therefore, they knew that they were not fit for the Kingdom of God, and well nigh ripe for destruction. The Spirit of the Lord fell upon Sidney, and he spoke with boldness, and he preached the gospel in its purity; but they laughed him to scorn, he being filled, with the Holy Spirit, he cried aloud O ye heavens give ere and ye angels attend, I bear witness in the name of Jesus Christ that this people is sealed up to everlasting destruction. And immediately he left them and escaped out of their hands. And his enemies were astonished and amazed at the doctrine which he preached, for they taught as men having authority and not as hireling priests.

After Joseph and Sidney returned from Colesville to Fayette. The Lord manifested himself to Joseph the Revelator and gave commandment for me [John Whitmer] to go to the Ohio, and carry the commandments and revelations, with me, to comfort and strengthen my brethren in that land.[17] The disciples had increased in number about three hundred. But the enemy of all righteous had got hold of Some of those who profesed to <be> his followers, because they had not sufficient knowledge to detect him in all his devices. He took anotion to blind the minds of some of the weaker ones, and made them think that an angel of God appeard to them, and showed them writings ond the outside cover of the Bible, and on parchment, which flew through the air, and on the back of their hands, and many such foolish and vain things. Others lost their strength, and some ~~scooted~~ <slid> ond the floor, and such like maneuvers, which proved greatly to the injury of the cause.[18]

The Lord also worked and many embraced the work, and the honest in heart stand firm and immovable. It was very [p. 11] nessary that this people should have instruction, and learn to decern between the things of God and the works of Satan. For the inhabitants of the earth knew nothing of the working of the Spirit of the Lord, in these days.

NOTES

1. Oliver Cowdery was born on October 3, 1806, in Wells, Rutland County, Vermont. He became acquainted with the Book of Mormon through stories he heard circulating in the Manchester, New York, area, where he was teaching school. Joseph Smith, Sr., the prophet's father, was one of the families who sent children to the school. Cowdery thus became acquainted with the Smith family and later went to board at their house. Here he became convinced of the divinity of the Book of Mormon plates and their contents and began writing as a scribe for their translation in April 1829. With Joseph Smith, Cowdery reported that he received the priesthood from angels a few months later. He also became one of the Three Witnesses to the Book of Mormon and a charter member of the church on April 6, 1830. He was the first scribe to assist Smith with his new translation of the Bible. On April 3, 1836, again with Smith, Cowdery received the keys of the priesthood from Elijah, Elias, and Moses as part of the Kirtland temple dedication ceremony.

Cowdery led the first proselyting mission to the Lamanites (American Indians) in the Missouri region in the winter of 1830-31, returning to Ohio in August 1831. He was ordained to the high priesthood on 29 August 1831 by Sidney Rigdon. Assigned the task of taking the money and text of the revelations to Missouri for publication, Cowdery was accompanied by John Whitmer. On December 18, 1832, Cowdery married Elizabeth Ann Whitmer, a sister of John Whitmer; they had six children.

Cowdery served on the Kirtland high council and assisted in administering church affairs during the summer of 1834 while Joseph Smith was in Missouri. He was ordained assistant president of the church on December 5, 1834, then returned to Missouri in 1837, arriving in Far West on October 20. Cowdery was excommunicated for apostasy on April 12, 1838, at Far West, Missouri. He went on to practice law in Ohio and Wisconsin. He was rebaptized by Orson Hyde on November 12, 1848. He died on March 3, 1850, while visiting David Whitmer in Missouri. See Cook, *Revelations*, 14; Anderson, *Witnesses*, 37-65; and *LDSBE*, 1:246-51.

2. Peter Whitmer, Jr., was born on September 27, 1809, at Fayette, New York, and baptized and ordained an elder by Oliver Cowdery sometime around June 9, 1830. One of the Eight Witnesses of the Book of Mormon, Peter was called on a proselyting mission to accompany Cowdery, Ziba Peterson, and Parley P. Pratt on the first Lamanite mission in Missouri. The group left New York sometime in the latter part of October 1830 and arrived in the Kirtland, Ohio, area by November 1. The group made a number of converts in the Kirtland area.

Whitmer and his fellow missionaries arrived in Independence, Jackson County, Missouri, on December 13, 1830. While there, Whitmer worked as a tailor. The group returned to Kirtland in October 1831.

Whitmer married Vashti Higley on October 14, 1832, in Jackson County, Missouri. The ceremony was performed by Oliver Cowdery. They had three children.

He died of tuberculosis near Liberty, Clay County, Missouri, on September 22, 1836 (Cook, *Revelations*, 26-27; *LDSBE*, 1:277).

3. Parley P. Pratt was born on April 12, 1807, in Burlington, Otsego County, New York. He married Thankful Halsey on September 9, 1827. They had one child: Parley Parker Pratt, Jr.

Parley, formerly a Campbellite minister, was baptized and ordained an elder in the LDS church in September 1830. He was appointed to travel with Oliver Cowdery, Peter Whitmer, Jr., and Ziba Peterson on the first Lamanite mission to Missouri in October 1830. The group left New York in late October, stopping over in Mentor, Ohio, about November 1. While in Mentor the group stopped at the home of Sidney Rigdon, a former Campbellite associate of Pratt, and presented him with a copy of the Book of Mormon. After baptizing Rigdon on November 14, 1830, and establishing a branch of the church in the area, the missionaries continued on to Missouri, arriving in Independence, Missouri, on December 13, 1830. Pratt returned to Kirtland, Ohio, about March 1, 1831, to make his report to the presidency of the church. In March 1831 he was called on a mission to the Shakers, then ordained a high priest on June 3.

Pratt returned to Jackson County, Missouri, as a resident in 1831. He was called as president of Branch Number Eight on September 11, 1833, and was sent in company with Lyman Wight to Kirtland on January 1, 1834, to counsel with the First Presidency on regaining church land in Jackson County. They arrived around February 24, 1834. The result of this trip was the organization of Zion's Camp, a Mormon militia, which marched to Missouri in 1834.

In 1836 Pratt participated in the dedication of the Kirtland temple. He was appointed a member of the Clay County high council on July 8, 1834, and on February 21, 1835, was ordained an apostle. He served several missions in 1835 to Pennsylvania, New York, and New England, and in 1836 to Toronto. In 1837-38 Pratt returned to New York on another mission. During this period he published his first LDS missionary tract, *A Voice of Warning.*

Pratt left on a proselyting mission to England with the rest of the Quorum of Twelve Apostles on August 29, 1839, arriving on April 6, 1840. While there he served as the first editor of *The Latter-day Saints' Millennial Star*, published in Manchester. In July 1840 he returned to the United States for his family before going back and resuming the editorial reins of the *Millennial Star*.

Pratt published a number of other church-related works in his lifetime, including the newspaper *The Prophet* in New York City (1844-45). He also composed hymns, many of which are found in the current LDS hymn book.

His first wife, Thankful Halsey, died on March 25, 1837. On May 9 Pratt married Mary Ann Frost. They had four children. He also married Elizabeth Brotherton on July 24, 1843; Mary Wood on September 9, 1844; Hannahette Snively on November 2, 1844; Belinda Marden, November 20, 1844; Sarah Huston, October 15, 1845; Phoebe Sopher, February 8, 1846; Martha Monks, April 28, 1847; Ann Agatha Walker, April 28, 1847; Keziah Downes, December 27, 1853; and Eleanor J. Macomb, November 14, 1855.

Pratt was called on a mission to the Southern States in December 1856. He was murdered by the jealous husband of one of his wives on May 13, 1857, in Van Buren, Crawford County, Arkansas (Cook, *Revelations*, 45-47; *LDSBE*, 1:83-85; see also Pratt, *Autobiography*).

4. Ziba Peterson was baptized on April 18, 1830, by Oliver Cowdery and ordained an elder sometime before June 9. He was appointed to accompany Oliver Cowdery, Peter Whitmer, Jr., and Parley P. Pratt on a proselyting mission to Missouri in October 1830. They arrived in Independence, Missouri, on December 13, 1830, and immediately found employment.

Peterson went with Peter Whitmer, Jr., to preach to Indians across the Missouri River on April 8, 1831, and later that month went with Oliver Cowdery to preach to anglo settlers residing in Lafayette County, Missouri.

Peterson was reprimanded for impropriety on August 1, 1831, made confession on the 4th, and married Rebecca Hopper, a convert from Lafayette County, Missouri, on the 11th.

Peterson became disaffected sometime early in 1833. He was excommunicated on June 25, 1833, and left Missouri for California with his family on May 3, 1848. He died in Placerville, Eldorado County, California, sometime after January but before June 1849 (Cook, *Revelations*, 45).

5. Joseph Smith, Jr., was born on December 23, 1805, in Sharon, Vermont, a son of Joseph Smith, Sr., and Lucy Mack Smith. At the age of ten, he moved with his family to the town of Palmyra, New York. Here he joined with his father and brothers in tending the family farm. From approximately September 1827 to mid-1829 he dictated the Book of Mormon, which he published in March 1830. The following April 6 he organized the Church of Christ. He married Emma Hale on January 18, 1827, in Harmony, Pennsylvania.

Controversy followed Smith wherever he went. Leaving New York for Ohio early in 1831, he and the rest of the Saints established new homes for themselves and a new headquarters for the church in Kirtland. Among the trials of the period, during the night of March 24, 1832, Smith and Sidney Rigdon were dragged from their homes, beaten, and tarred and feathered.

The prophet and some other leaders left for Missouri in January 1838. Joseph and his family settled in the town of Far West. Before long the so-called "Mormon War" of 1838-39 erupted between Mormons and units of the state militia. Along with other prominent church members, Smith was arrested for treason, murder, arson, and other charges. He, his brother Hyrum, Sidney Rigdon, and several others were incarcerated for the winter in the town of Liberty, Missouri. The next April he and fellow prisoners escaped while being transferred to another jail. They made their way east and joined the rest of the church in Quincy, Illinois, several days later.

In Illinois the church purchased the boggy townsite of Commerce, Hancock County, renaming it "Nauvoo." Smith, who had passed the bar in Missouri and was studying for the

Illinois bar, was elected mayor in 1842, succeeding John C. Bennett who had left the church. Smith held this office until his death in 1844. When the Nauvoo Legion, the city's militia, was organized in 1841, Smith served as a lieutenant general. Before the Mormons left Illinois in 1846, the legion contained over 2,000 men, which was a constant source of worry to the non-Mormon population of the county.

It was the combination of independent civil and military power, along with rumors of polygamy, aggravated by the city council's order to destroy the town's anti-Mormon newspaper, the *Nauvoo Expositor*, that led to the deaths of Joseph and Hyrum Smith in Carthage Jail on June 27, 1844 (Donna Hill, *Joseph Smith: The First Mormon* [Garden City, NY: Doubleday, 1977]; *LDSBE*, I:1-8).

6. D&C 32; see also *HC*, 1:118-25. For a more complete history of the mission and the church in Kirtland, see Backman, *Heavens*, 1-19; James B. Allen and Glen M. Leonard, *The Story of the Latter-day Saints*, 2d ed. rev. (Salt Lake City: Deseret Book Co., 1992), 61-111; Max H. Parkin, "Conflict at Kirtland: A Study of the Nature and Causes of External and Internal Conflict of the Mormons in Ohio Between 1830 and 1838," M.A. thesis, Brigham Young University, 1966, 33-46; and Larry O. Porter, "Origins of the Church of Jesus Christ of Latter-day Saints in New York and Pennsylvania, 1816-1831," Ph.D. diss., Brigham Young University, 277-85.

Pratt described the results of their efforts among the Indians as follows:

> We continued for several days to instruct the old chief [of the Delaware tribe] and many of his tribe. The interest became more and more intense on their part, from day to day, until at length nearly the whole tribe began to feel a spirit of inquiry and excitement on the subject.
>
> We found several among them who could read, and to them we gave copies of the Book [of Mormon], explaining to them that it was the Book of their forefathers.
>
> Some began to rejoice exceedingly, and took great pains to tell

the news to others, in their own language.

The excitement now reached the frontier settlements in Missouri, and stirred up the jealousy and envy of the Indian agents and sectarian missionaries to that degree that we were soon ordered out of the Indian country as disturbers of the peace; and even threatened with the military in case of non-compliance.

We accordingly departed from the Indian country, and came over the line [into Missouri from Kansas], and commenced laboring in Jackson County, Missouri, among the whites. We were well received, and listened to by many; and some were baptized and added to the Church.

Thus ended our first Indian Mission, in which we had preached the gospel in its fulness, and distributed the record of their forefathers among three tribes, viz: the Catteraugus Indians, near Buffalo, N.Y., the Wyandots of Ohio, and the Delawares west of Missouri (Pratt, *Autobiography*, 44).

After the call issued in the revelation was confirmed by a church conference at the Whitmer home in Fayette from September 26, 1830, through early October, the missionaries left New York in late October, arriving in the Kirtland area early in November. After establishing a branch of the church, they left for Missouri the first part of January 1831 and arrived sometime later that month. Shortly after they settled in the Jackson County region, Parley P. Pratt was chosen by the group to go back to Kirtland and make a report to Joseph Smith on the progress of their mission. Pratt left in late February and arrived sometime in early March 1831, returning to Missouri in June.

7. Sidney Rigdon was born on February 19, 1793, in St. Clair Township, Alleghany County, Pennsylvania. He joined the Regular Baptists and received a license to preach in March 1819, moving to Warren, Ohio, in May. He married Phoebe Brook on June 12, 1820. They became the parents of eleven children.

In 1822 the Baptists of Pittsburgh appointed Rigdon as their minister. He held that post until August 1824 when he informed the congregation that he could no longer uphold the doctrines they taught. He labored as a tanner with his brother-in-law from

1824-26.

He was again invited to become a minister, this time to the Regular Baptist church in Bainbridge, Geauga County, Ohio, in 1826. A year later, in 1827, he accepted a similar call in Mentor, Ohio.

It was in Mentor where Rigdon finally broke with the Baptists completely. With other major religious figures in the nineteenth century, such as Walter Scott and Alexander Campbell, Rigdon believed remission of sins and reception of the Holy Ghost followed baptism by immersion. Fellowship was withdrawn by the Mentor church in September 1828 for Rigdon's "novel notions." Shortly afterwards he joined with Alexander Campbell in a movement that later became known as the Disciples of Christ or "Campbellites."

Rigdon was living in Mentor when Mormon missionaries first arrived in November 1830. Parley P. Pratt, a former associate in the Campbellite ministry, introduced him to the Book of Mormon. Rigdon was baptized on November 14, 1830. In December he traveled to Fayette, New York, to meet Joseph Smith and became completely devoted to him. He served as the prophet's scribe for most of the work on the revision of the Bible. In February 1831 Rigdon returned to Ohio.

On June 3, 1831, Rigdon was ordained a high priest. Shortly after that he accompanied the prophet to Independence, Missouri, arriving in late July. Here on August 2 they dedicated the "land of Zion" for the gathering of the Saints.

Rigdon was ordained to the presidency of the high priesthood on March 8, 1832, and left for Missouri again in April with Smith to regulate the affairs of the church there. They returned to Kirtland on May 26, 1832. Rigdon temporarily lost his position in the High Priesthood during the summer of 1832 after preaching that the kingdom had been taken from the Saints due to Smith's avarice; he was restored to his former office shortly afterwards. On March 18, 1833, he was ordained as a counselor in the First Presidency.

When Rigdon and Smith were dragged from their homes in

Kirtland on March 24, 1831, Rigdon was tied to the back of a horse by his heels and dragged along the frozen ground, severely injuring his head (*HC*, 1:261-65.)

Rigdon made many trips with the prophet, including one to Upper Canada in 1833 and to Massachusetts that fall, then back to Massachusetts again in 1836. He accompanied Smith and others to Washington, D.C., in 1839-40 to present Congress with petitions of redress for losses suffered in Missouri in 1838-39.

Along with Smith, Rigdon was also prominent in church business enterprises, such as the Kirtland Safety Society Anti-Banking Corporation in 1837. He assisted in founding Nauvoo in 1840, became a City Attorney, a member of the Nauvoo City Council, and the city's Postmaster. He was chosen as Smith's U.S. vice-presidential candidate in 1844.

In a way, Rigdon helped precipitate the Mormon War in Missouri of 1838-39 through his famous "Salt Sermon" in June 1838 and his 4th of July 1838 sermon. In these he threatened apostates and effectively declared war on outside antagonists. These remarks lit the fuse of an already explosive situation and provided motivation for Danite maneuvers on the part of Mormons and militia attacks through the next year on the part of non-Mormon neighbors and politicians.

After Smith was murdered in June 1844, Rigdon, in a church conference on August 8, claimed his right to act as "guardian of the Church" until Smith's son was grown. He was rejected by the majority of the Saints, who chose instead to follow Brigham Young and the Council of Twelve Apostles. Rigdon was subsequently excommunicated on September 8. Shortly afterwards he moved to Pittsburgh and organized his own church, the Church of Christ, based on the Book of Mormon and teachings of Joseph Smith. It lasted from 1844-46. He organized a second church in 1863, the Church of Jesus of the Children of Zion. It lasted until about 1883. He and his wife were thereafter cared for by their children in Friendship, New York. He died there on July 14, 1876 (Cook, *Revelations*, 52-53, 129-30; Daryl Chase,

"Sidney Rigdon: Early Mormon," M.A. thesis, University of Chicago, 1931; F. Mark McKiernan, *The Voice of One Crying in the Wilderness: Sidney Rigdon, Religious Reformer, 1793-1876* [Lawrence, KS: Coronado Press, 1971]; Richard S. Van Wagoner, *Sidney Rigdon: A Portrait of Religious Excess* [Salt Lake City: Signature Books, 1994]; Thomas J. Gregory, "Sidney Rigdon: Post-Nauvoo," *Brigham Young University Studies* 21 (Winter 1981):51-67; *LDSBE*, 1:31-34; Steven L. Shields, *Divergent Paths of the Restoration*, 4th rev. ed. [Los Angeles, CA: Restoration Research, 1990], 36-39).

8. Edward Partridge was born on August 27, 1793, in Pittsfield, Massachusetts. In 1813, after completing four years as an apprentice, he became a journeyman hatter in Clinton, New York. He later moved to Painesville, Ohio, where he owned a hatting business. He married Lydia Clisbee on August 22, 1819. He joined the Campbellites in 1828, then in November 1830 attended meetings held in the Kirtland, Ohio, area by the LDS missionaries headed for Missouri. He accompanied Sidney Rigdon on a trip back to New York in early December to meet the prophet Joseph Smith—the trip mentioned by Whitmer in this manuscript. Satisfied with what he found, Partridge was baptized on December 11, 1830. On December 15 he was ordained an elder. He immediately left on a two-month mission to relatives in Massachusetts, returning to Ohio by February 4, 1831. He also went on a mission to the Eastern states, serving from June 2 to November 3, 1835.

On February 4, 1831, at a special conference, Partridge was ordained the first bishop in the church and a high priest on June 3, 1831. Appointed to travel to Missouri with the Prophet in June 1831, he was then directed to move his family there that August. The family settled in Jackson County, and Partridge, as bishop of the church in Zion, became responsible for administering the communal Law of Consecration. He was acknowledged as presiding officer of the church in Missouri on September 11, 1833, and remained so until the appointment of a presidency for the church in Missouri and a high council in June 1834. Accompanied by Thomas B. Marsh, Partridge traveled to Kirtland from January 27 through April 29, 1835, to receive his temple endowment. He received his patriarchal blessing from Joseph Smith, Sr., on May 4, 1835. In 1836 Partridge participated in the dedication of the Kirtland temple, returning to Missouri later that summer.

Partridge, who had been tarred and feathered during the night of July 20, 1833, moved his family from Jackson County to Clay County in November 1833, then to the city of Far West in the fall of 1836. He was incarcerated in November 1838 for treason, though never convicted. After his release, Partridge joined his family in Quincy, Illinois, in January 1839 and settled in Nauvoo during that summer. On October 5, 1839, at the church's general conference, Partridge was appointed bishop of the upper ward in Nauvoo. He served in this calling until his death on May 27, 1840, in Nauvoo (Cook, *Revelations*, 53-54; *LDSBE*, 1:218-22).

    9. D&C 35. For historical background and revelatory process, see Cook, *Revelations*, 51-53, 129-30. Whitmer follows the 1833 text of the Book of Commandments, where this revelation appears as Chapter 37. Compare Wood, 2[1833]:75-78, for text.

    10. See *HC*, 1:131-39. The "Prophecy of Enoch" is currently included as Moses 7 in the LDS edition of the Pearl of Great Price. The Book of Moses consists of a revelation given to Moses concerning the creation of the world, the fall of Adam and Eve, and the ministries of Abraham, Noah, and Enoch. See H. Donl Peterson, *The Pearl of Great Price: A History and Commentary* (Salt Lake City: Deseret Book Co., 1987), 3-35.

    11. D&C 37; compare Wood, 2[1833]:79-80, where it was published as Chapter 39. For background, see Cook, *Revelations*, 54-55, 130.

    12. See *Far West Record*, 5; and *HC*, 1:140-43. The date for

the meeting in both sources is January 2, 1831.

13. D&C 37.

14. D&C 38; compare Wood, 2[1833]:80-84, where this section was published as Chapter 40, and Cook, *Revelations*, 55-56, 130, for historical background.

15. Exactly what the threat was that motivated the move to Ohio is not certain. However, it is significant to note that due to the growth of the church in Kirtland because of the efforts of Parley P. Pratt and his companions as they were on their way to their mission in Missouri in 1831, a relatively large community of believers was ready in the Kirtland area to receive the New York Saints, whereas Joseph Smith's and others' preaching had created opponents around Fayette, Palmyra, and other parts of the state. See Backman, *Heavens*, 1-51.

16. Colesville's first connection with the church was in 1826, when Joseph Smith was hired as a farmhand by Joseph Knight, Sr. The entire Knight family eventually converted to Mormonism and provided a base of support for Joseph Smith and other missionaries in the area. When the church left New York for Ohio in 1831, the Colesville Branch moved as a body and settled as a body in Kirtland. The branch maintained its corporate identity until 1836, when, following the exodus of the Saints from Clay County, Missouri, into Caldwell and other counties in the state, the members of the Colesville Branch were finally absorbed by local Missouri branches. See Porter, "Origins," 181-86, 195-222, 296-311.

17. This may be a reference to the revelation now included in D&C 69. That revelation instructed Oliver Cowdery to take the revelations to Missouri for publication and to take Whitmer as a traveling companion. No mention is made of stopping in Ohio.

18. For a summary of these incidents, see Backman, *Heavens*,

59-62; and Parkin, "Conflict at Kirtland," 66-76. George Albert Smith later recalled these events as follows:

> There was at this time in Kirtland, a society that had undertaken to have a community of property; it has sometimes been denominated the Morley family, as there was a number of them located on a farm owned by Captain Isaac Morley. These persons had been baptized, but had not yet been instructed in relation to their duties. A false spirit entered into them, developing their singular, extravagant and wild ideas. They had a meeting at the farm, and among them was a negro known generally as Black Pete, who became a revelator. Others also manifested wonderful developments; they could see angels, and letters would come down from heaven, they said, and they would be put through wonderful unnatural distortions. Finally on one occasion, Black Pete got sight of one of those revelations carried by a black angel, he started after it, and ran off a steep wash bank twenty-five feet high, passed through a tree top into the Chagrin river beneath. He came out with a few scratches, and his ardor somewhat cooled.
>
> Joseph Smith came to Kirtland, and taught that people in relation to their error. He showed them that the Spirit of God did not bind men nor make them insane, and that the power of the adversary which had been manifested in many instances was visible even from that cause, for persons under its influence became helpless, and were bound hand and foot as in chains, being as immovable as a stick of timber (*Journal of Discourses*, 26 vols. [Liverpool, Eng.: Latter-day Saints' Book Depot, 1855-86; reprint ed., n.p., 1966], 11:3-4).

Chapter 2
A Paid Ministry

CHAPTER II

About these days Joseph the Prophet and Sidney arrived at Kirtland to the joy and satisfaction of the Saints.[1] The disciples had all things common, and were going to destruction very fast as to temporal things: for they considered from reading the scripture that what belonged to a brother belonged to any of the brethren, therefore they would take each others clothes and other property and use it without leave: which brought on confusion and disappointments. for they did not under stand the scripture.[2] After Joseph lived here a few days the word of the Lord came saying[3]:

> Hearken and hear O ye my people, saith the Lord and your God, ye whom I delight to bless with the greatest blessings; ye that hear me; and ye that hear me not will I curse, that have professed my name, with the heav[i]est of all cursings. Hearken O ye Elders of my church whom I have called, behold I give unto you a commandment, that you shall assemble yourselves together to agree upon my word, and by the prayer of your faith ye shall receive my law, that ye may

D&C 41

Shows possible pre-B.C. alterations

know how to govern my church, and have all things right before me.

And I will be your Ruler when I come: and behold I come quickly; and ye shall see that my law is kept. He that receiveth my law and doeth it the same is my desciple; and he that saith he receiveth my law and doeth it not is not my desciple, and shall be cast out from among you, for it is not meet that the things which belong to the children of the kingdom should be given to them that are not worthy, or to dogs, or the pearl to be cast before Swine.

And again, it is meet that my servant Joseph Smith Jr. should have a house built, in which to live and translate. And again, [p. 12] it is meet that my Servant Sidney should live as seemeth him good, inasmuch as he keepeth my commandments. And again I have called my servant Edward Partridge, and give a commandment, that he should be appointed by the voice of the church, and ordained a bishop, unto the church, to leave his merchandise and to spend all his time in the labors of the church; to see to all things as it shall be appointed unto him, in my laws in the day that I shall give them. And this because his heart is pure before me, for he is like Nathaniel of old, in whom there is no guile. These words are given unto you, and they are pure before me, wherefore beware how you hold them, for they are to be answered upon your souls in the day of Judgment; even so: Amen.

Behold after this revelation was receiv[e]d the Elders were called together, and, united in mighty prayer, and were agreed as touching the reception of the Law[4]: therefore; Thus Saith the Lord: ~~your~~ ~~God,~~ even Jesus ~~Christ,~~ ~~the~~ ~~Great~~ I ~~AM,~~ Hearken, O ye E[l]ders of my church who have assembled themselves together, in my name, even Jesus Christ, the Son of the Living God, the Savior of the world; inasmuch as they believe on my name and keep my commandments; again, I say unto you, hearken and hear and obey the law which I shall give unto you: for verily I say, as ye have assembled yourselves together, according to the commandment wherewith I commanded you, and are agreed as touching this one thing, and have asked the Father in my name, even so ye shall receive.

Behold, verily I say unto you, I give unto you this first commandment, that ye shall go forth in my name, every one of you, excepting my servant Joseph Smith Jr. and Sidney Rigdon. And I give unto them a commandment, that they shall go forth for a little season, and it shall be given by the power of the Spirit when they shall return, and ye shall go forth in the power of my Spirit, preaching my gospel, two by two, in my name, lifting up your voices as with the voice of a trump declaring my word like unto angels of God: and ye shall go [p. 13] forth baptizing with water, saying: Repent ye, repent ye, for the Kingdom of heaven is at hand.

And from this place ye shall go forth into the regions westward, and inasmuch as ye will find them that will believe you, ye shall build up my church in every region, until the time shall come when it shall be revealed unto you, from on high, when the City of the New Jerusalem shall be prepared that ye may be gathered in one, that ye may be my people and I will be your God. And again, I say unto you, that my Servant Edward Partridge shall stand in the office wherewith I have appointed him. And it shall come to pass, that if he transgress, another shall be planted in his stead; even so. Amen.

Again I say unto you, that it shall not be given to any one to go forth to preach my gospel, or to build up my church, except he be ordained by some one who has authority, and has been regularly ordained by the heads of the church.

And again, the Elders, Priests and Teachers of this church,

shall teach the principles of my gospel which are in the Bible and the book of Mormon, in the which is the fulness of the gospel; and they shall observe the covenants and church articles to do them, and these shall be their teachings, as they shall be directed, by the Spirit: and the Spirit shall be given unto you by the prayer of faith, and if ye receive not the Spirit ye shall not teach. And all this ye shall observe to do as I have commanded, concerning your teaching, until the fulness of my scripture are given.

And as you shall lift up your voices by the Comforter, ye shall speak and prophesy as seemeth me good; for behold the Comforter knoweth all things, and beareth record of the Father and of the Son.

And now, behold I speak unto the church: Thou shalt not kill, and he that kills shall not have forgiveness, in this world nor in the world to come.

And again, I say, thou shalt not kill, but he that killeth shall die. Thou shalt not steal, and he that stealeth and will not [p. 14] repent, shall be cast out. Thou shalt not lie; he that lieth and will not repent, shall be cast out. Thou shalt love thy wife with all thy heart, and shalt cleave unto her with all and none else; and he that looketh upon a woman to lust after her, shall deny the faith, and shall not have the Spirit, and if he repents not, he shall be cast out. Thou shalt not commit adultery; and he that has committeth adultery and repenteth not, shall be cast out; but he that committed adultery and repents with all his heart, and forsaketh it and doeth it no more, thou shalt forgive; but if he doeth it again, he shall not be forgiven, but shall be cast out. Thou shalt not speak evil of thy neighbor, nor do him any harm. Thou knowest my laws concerning these things are given in my Scriptures: he that sinneth and repenteth not, shall be cast out.

If thou lovest me, thou shalt serve me and keep all my commandments. And behold, thou wilt remember the poor, and consecrate of thy properties for their support, that which thou hast to impart unto them, with a covenant and a deed which cannot be broken and inasmuch as ye impart of your substance unto the poor, ye will do it unto me, and they shall be laid before the Bishop of my church, and his counsellors, two of the elders, or high priests such as he shall or has appointed and set apart for that purpose.

And it shall come to pass, that after they are laid before the Bishop of my church, and after that he has received these testimonies, concerning the consecration of the properties of my church, that they cannot be taken from the church, agreeable to my commandments, every man shall be made accountable unto me, a steward over his own property, or that which he has received by consecration, inasmuch as is sufficient for himself and family.

And again, if there <shall be> properties in the hands of the church, or any individuals of it, more than is necessary for their support, after this first consecration, which is a residue, to be conse [p. 15] crated unto the bishop, it shall be kept to administer to those who have not, from time to time, that every man who hath need may be amply supplied, and receive according to his wants. Therefore, the residue shall be kept in my storehouse, to administer to the poor and the needy, as shall be appointed by the high counsel of the church, and for the purpose of purchasing lands for the public benefit of the church, and building houses of worship, and building up the New Jerusalem which is hereafter to be revealed, that my covenant people may be gathered in one in the day when I shall come to my temple. And this I do for the salvation of my people.

And it shall come to pass, that he that sinneth and repenteth not, shall be cast out of the church, and shall not receive again that which he has consecrated unto the poor and the needy of my church, or in other words unto me. for inasmuch as ye do it unto the least of these ye do it unto me—for it shall come to pass, that which I spake by the mouths of my prophets, shall be fulfilled; for I will consecrate of the riches of those who embrace my gospel among the Gentiles, unto the poor of my people who are of the house of Israel.

And again thou shalt not be proud in thy heart, let all thy garments be plain, and their beauty the beauty of the work of thine own hands, and let all things be done in cleanliness before me. Thou shalt not be idle, for he that is idle shall not eat the bread, or wear the garments of the laborer. And whomsoever among [them] that are sick, and have not faith to be healed, but believe, shall be nourished with all tenderness with herbs and mild food, and that not by the hand of an enemy. And the elders of the church, two or more, shall be called, and shall pray for and lay their hands upon them and if they die they shall die unto me, and if they live they shall live unto me. Thou shalt live together in love, insomuch that thou shalt weep for the loss of them that die, and more especially for those who <that> have not hope of a glorious resurrection. And it shall come to pass, that those that die in me, shall not taste of [p. 16] death, for it shall be sweet unto them; and they that die not in me, woe unto them for their death is bitter.

And again, it shall come to pass, that he that has faith in me, to be healed, and is not appointed unto death, shall be healed: he who has faith to see shall see: he who has faith to hear shall hear: the lame who have faith to leap shall leap: and they who have not faith to do these things, but believe in me, have power to become my sons: and inasmuch as they break not my laws, thou shalt bear their infirmities.

Thou shalt stand in the place of thy stewardship: thou shalt not take thy brother's garment; thou shalt pay for that which thou shalt receive of thy brother; and if thou obtainest more than that which would be for thy support, thou shalt give it in my storehouse, that all things may be done according to that which I have said.

Thou shalt ask, and my scriptures shall be given as I have appointed, and they shall be preserved in safety; and it is expedient that thou shouldest hold thy peace concerning them, and not teach them until ye have received them in full. And I give unto you a commandment, that then ye shall teach them unto all men; for they shall be taught unto all nations, kindreds, tongues and people.

Thou shalt take the things which thou hast received, which have been given unto thee in my Scriptures for a law, to be my law, to govern my church; and he that doeth according to these things, shall be saved, and he that doeth them not shall be damned, if he continue.

If thou shalt ask, thou shalt receive revelation upon revelation; knowledge upon knowledge; that thou mayest know the mysteries and peaceable things; that which bringeth joy, that which bringeth life eternal. Thou shalt ask and it shall be revealed unto you in mine own due time, where the New Jerusalem shall be built.

And behold it shall come to pass, that my servants shall be sent forth to the east, and to the west, to the north and to the South; and even now, let him that goeth to the east, teach them that shall be converted to flee to the west, and this in [p. 17] consequence of that which is coming on the earth, and of secret combinations. Behold thou shalt observe all these things, and great shall be thy reward; for unto you it is given to know the mysteries of the kingdom, but unto the world it is not given to know them. Ye shall observe the laws which ye have received, and be faithful. And ye shall hereafter receive church covenants, such as shall be sufficient to establish you, both here and in the New Jerusalem. Therefore, he that lacketh wisdom let him ask of me, and I will give him liberally, and upbraid him not. Lift up your hearts and rejoice, for unto you the kingdom, or in other words, the keys of the church, have been given; even so. Amen.

The priests and teachers shall have their stewardships, even as the members, and the elders or high priests, who are appointed to assist the bishop as counsellors, in all things are to have their families supported out of their propertys which is consecrated to the bishop, for the good of the poor, and for other purposes, as before mentioned; or they are to receive a ~~stewardship~~ just remuneration for all their services; either a stewardship, or otherwise, as may be thought best or decided by the counsellors and bishop. And the bishop also, shall receive his support or a just remuneration for all his services in the Church.

NOTES

1. Joseph Smith, Sidney Rigdon, Edward Partridge, and their families arrived on or about February 1, 1831 (*HC*, 1:145-46; Backman, *Heavens*, 44-45).

2. For the Mormon experiment with communalism, see Backman, *Heavens*, 64-66; Max H. Parkin, "Conflict at Kirtland: A Study of the Nature and Causes of External and Internal Conflict of the Mormons in Ohio Between 1830 and 1838," M.A. thesis, Brigham Young University, 1966, 35-36. Christian

communal groups abounded during this time. Many groups, such as the Campbellites and the Shakers, felt it was necessary for the true saints of God to share their worldly possessions as outlined in Acts 4:32-37 to prepare for the Lord's coming. (See Michael Barkun, *Crucible of the Millennium: The Burned-Over District of New York in the 1840s* [Syracuse, NY: Syracuse University Press, 1986], 63-88; Sydney E. Ahlstrom, *A Religious History of the American People* [New Haven: Yale University Press, 1972], 491-509; Whitney R. Cross, *The Burned-Over District: The Social and Intellectual History of Enthusiastic Religion in Western New York, 1800-1850* [Ithaca, NY: Cornell University Press, 1950], 322-40.)

3. D&C 41; compare Wood, 2[1833]:88-89, for original published text. For background, see Cook, *Revelations*, 57-59, 131.

4. D&C 42:1-73; compare Wood, 2[1833]:89-95 (Book of Commandments, 44:1-54). The 1833 text contains three additional verses which are not included in Whitmer's history. Whitmer apparently used a different source, either a clerk's copy or a copy derived from the clerk's text, and made an exception to his practice of following the Book of Commandments.

This revelation was the first endorsement and modification of Rigdon's pre-Mormon communal structure at two locations. Mormons in Kirtland organized the United Order, a joint-stock firm to which the Saints subscribed. Later, in Missouri, the "Law of Consecration" would be practiced on a truly communal basis, with all private property donated and deeded to the church through the bishop. The bishop in turn deeded back to donors what they needed to live. Those with surpluses gave them to the bishop who kept them in a storehouse for the poor (Cook, *Revelations*, 59-61, 131-32; and *Joseph Smith and the Law of Consecration* [Provo, UT: Grandin Book, 1985]; Backman, *Heavens*, 63-81; James B. Allen and Glen M. Leonard, *The Story of the Latter-day Saints*, 2d rev. ed. [Salt Lake City: Deseret Book Co., 1992], 84-88).

Chapter 3
Competing Prophets

CHAPTER III

After the above law or Revelation was received the elders went forth to proclaim repentance according to commandment, and there were numbers added to the church. The Bishop Edward Partridge visited the church in its several branches, there were some that would not receive the Law. The time has not yet come that the law can be fully established, for the disciples live scattered abroad and are not organized, our numbers are small, and the disciples untaught, consequently they understand not the things of the Kingdom. There were some of the disciples who were flattered into the church because [p. 18] they thought that all things were to be common, therefore they thought to glut themselves upon the labors of others.

About these days there was a woman by the name of Hubble who professed to be a prophetess of the Lord and professed to have many revelations, and knew ~~that~~ the Book of Mormon was true; and that she should become a teacher in the Church of Christ. She appear[ed] very sanctimonious and deceived some, who were not able to detect her in her hypocracy: others however had a spirit of dicernment; and her folies and abominations were made manifest.[1] The Lord gave Revelation that the saints might not be deceived which reads as follows.[2]

O hearken, ye elders of my church, and give ere [ear] to the words which I shall speak unto you; for behold, verily, verily, I say unto you, that ye have received a commandment for a law unto my church, through him whom I have appointed unto you, to receive commandments and revelations from my hand. And this ye shall know assuredly, that there is none other appointed unto you to receive <commandments and> revelations until he be taken if he abide in me.

But verily, verily I say unto you, that none else shall be appointed unto this gift except it be through him, for if it be taken from him he shall not have power, except to appoint another in his stead: and this shall be a law unto you, that ye receive not the teachings of any that shall come before you as revelations or commandments: and this I give unto you that you may not be deceivd; that you may know they are not of me. For verily I say unto you, that he that is ordained of me shall come in at the gate and be ordained as I told you before, to teach those revelations which you have received, and shall receive through him whom I have appointed.

And now, Behold I ~~say unto you~~ I give unto you a commandment, [p. 19] that when ye are assembled together, ye shall instruct and edify each other, that ye may know how to act and instruct my church how to act upon the points of my law and commandments, which I have given: and thus ye shall become instructed in the law of my church, and be sanctified by that which ye have received, and ye shall bind yourselves to act in all holiness before me, that inasmuch as ye do this, glory shall be added to the kingdom which ye have received. Purge ye out the iniquity that is among you; sanctify yourselves before me and if ye desire the glories of the kingdom, appoint ye my Servant Joseph Smith Jr. and uphold him before me by the prayer of faith. And again, I say unto you, that if ye desire the mysteries of the kingdom, provide for him food and raiment and whatsoever he needeth to accomplish the work, wherewith I have commanded him: and if ye do it not, he shall remain unto them who have received him, that I may reserve unto myself a pure people before me.

Again I say, hearken ye elders of my church, whom I have appointed: ye are not appointed <sent forth> to be taught, but to teach the children of men the things which I have put into your hands by the power of my Spirit: and ye are <to be> taught from on high. Sanctify yourselves and ye shall be endowed with power, that ye may give even as I have spoken.

Hearken ye, for behold the great day of the Lord is near at hand. For the day cometh that the Lord shall utter his voice out of heaven; the heavens shall shake and the earth shall tremble, and the trump of God shall sound both long and loud, and shall say to the sleeping nations: Ye saints arise and live: Ye sinners stay and sleep until I shall call again; wherefore gird up your loins, lest ye be found among the wicked. Lift up your voices and spare not. Call upon the nations to repent, both old and young, both bond and free; saying, Prepare yourselves, for the great day of the Lord; for if I who am a man, do lift up my voice and call upon you to [p. 20] repent, and ye hate me, what will ye say when the day cometh when the thunders shall utter their voices from the ends of the earth speaking to the ears of all that live, saying repent, and prepare, for the great day of the Lord? Yea, and again, when the lightnings shall streak forth from the east to the west, and shall utter forth their voices unto all that live, and make the ears of all tingle, that hear these words saying, Repent ye for the great day of the Lord is come.

And again, the Lord shall utter his voice out of heaven saying: Hearken, O ye nations of the earth, and hear the words of that God who made you. O ye nations of the earth, how often I would have gathered you together as a hen gathereth her chicken under her wings, but ye would not?

How oft have I called upon you by the mouth of my Servants; and by the ministering of angels; and by mine own voice; and by the voice of thunderings; and by the voice of lightnings; and by the voice of tempests; and by the voice of earthquakes; and great hailstorms; and by the voice of famines, and pestilence of every kind; and by the great sound of a trump; and by the voice of Judgement; and by the voice of mercy all the day long, and by the voice of glory, and honor, and the riches of eternal life; and would have saved you with an everlasting salvation, but ye would not! Behold the day has come, when the cup of the wrath of mine indignation is full.

Behold, verily I say unto you, that these are the words of the Lord your God; Wherefore, labor ye, labor ye, in my vineyard for the last time; for the last time call upon the inhabitants of the earth, for in my own due time it will come upon the earth in Judgment, and my people shall be redeemed, and shall reign with me on earth; for the great Millennium, which I have spoken by the mouth of my servants, shall come; for Satan shall be bound; and when he is loosed again he shall only reign for a little season, [p. 21] and then cometh the end of the earth: and he that liveth in righteouness, shall be changed in the twinkling of an eye; and the earth shall pass away so as by fire; and the wicked shall go away into unquenchable fire; and their end no man knoweth, on earth nor ever shall know, until they come before me into judgment.

Hearken ye to these words; behold I am Jesus Christ the Savior of the World. Treasure these things up in your hearts, and let the solemnities rest upon your minds. Be sober. Keep all the commandments: even so: Amen.

After this commandment was received the saints came to understanding on this subject, and unity and harmony prevailed throughout the church of God: and the Saints began to learn wisdom, and treasure up knowledge which they learned from the word of God, and by experience as they advanced in the way of eternal life. And Joseph Smith J. the Seer continued the translation of the holy Scriptures.[3] And the word of the Lord came to Joseph Smith Junior: Saying[4]: Behold thus saith the Lord, unto you my Servants, it is expedient in me that the elders of my Church should be called together: from the east, and from the west from the north and from the South by letter or otherwise. And it shall come to pass that I will pour out my Spirit upon them in the day that they assemble themselves together; and it shall come to pass, that they shall go forth unto the regions round about; and preach repentance unto this people, and many shall be converted, insomuch that ye shall obtain power to organize yourselves, according to the laws of man, that your enemies may be under your feet in all things; that ye may be enabled to keep my laws, that every band may be broken wherewith the enemy seeketh to bind you. Behold I say unto you, that you must visit the poor and the needy, and administer unto their relief, that they may be kept until all things may be done according to my law which ye have received. Amen.

The translation [of the Bible] continued: And the elders were sent for according to the preceeding Revelation.

[p. 22] <March> June 4, 1831.[5] This was a day appointed for a general Conference. from whence the elders were sent forth to preach the gospel and many were added of such as were determined to be saved.

About this time some were sick of various diseases, and were healed by the power which was in them through Jesus Christ.

There was a tradition among some of the disciples, that those who obeyed the covenant in the last days, would never die: but by experience, they have learned to the contrary.[6]

In those days the Lord blessed his disciples greatly, and he gave Revelation after Revelation, which contained doctrine, instructions, and prophecies: The word of the Lord came to the Seer as follows: "published in the edition of book of doctrine and covenants published at Kirtland Ohio, 1835. Page 128. Insert the Revelation."[7]

Some of the Elders returned from their missions, to gain some rest and instructions. They rehearsed some of the wickedness which they had seen among this generation: while they were proclaiming the gospel, and warning the people, some would cry false prophets, false christ &c. Some would receive the word gladly until their priests would cry delusion! delusion!! for this generation abounds with priests, which they have heaped up unto themselves, and every one is teaching for hire: consequently every one is looking for his gain from his quarter. They will persecute the disciples, and cause their followers to do likewise. Out of the mixed multitude some obey the gospel of peace and bring forth fruit some an hundred fold.

The Lord is pouring forth some of his judgments, in token of the last days. An earthquake in *China* destroyed about one Million of souls. But judgments in these days as in former days serves to harden men, until it is to[o] late to repent.[8]

NOTES

1. Hubble was one of a number of early members who claimed revelation for the church (Backman, *Heavens*, 59-62;

Pratt, *Autobiography*, 48-52; Max H. Parkin, "Conflict at Kirtland: A Study of the Nature and Causes of External and Internal Conflict of the Mormons in Ohio Between 1830 and 1838," M.A. thesis, Brigham Young University, 1966, 11-16, 66-81; and, in particular, George A. Smith in *Journal of Discourses*, 26 vols. [Liverpool, Eng.: Latter-day Saints' Book Depot, 1855-86; reprint ed., n.p., 1966], 11:2-8, hereafter cited as *JD*). They represented the enthusiastic strain of American religion, which promoted physical manifestations of the Spirit (see David S. Lovejoy, *Religious Enthusiasm in the New World, Heresy to Revolution* [Cambridge, MA: Harvard University Press, 1985]; and Whitney R. Cross, *The Burned-Over District: The Social and Intellectual History of Enthusiastic Religion in Western New York, 1800-1850* [Ithaca, NY: Cornell University Press, 1950]).

2. D&C 43; compare Wood, 2[1833]:96-100, for the original published text, where it was published as Chapter 45. For background, see Cook, *Revelations*, 61-62, 132.

3. In June 1830 Joseph Smith began working on what he referred to as a "new translation" of the Bible. Believing that a number of scriptural passages had suffered through the process of repeated copying and translating over the centuries, Joseph attempted to restore these verses by revelation to the original intent of their ancient authors. He ended the major part of his effort in 1833, "sealing up" his work until such time as it could be taken to Missouri for publication. Unfortunately, because of the pressures of anti-Mormon mobs and other problems Joseph never published the work while he was alive; indeed, he kept making corrections and amendations in it until shortly before he was killed. (For a history of the translation process and the status of Joseph's work today, see Robert J. Mathews, *"A Plainer Translation": Joseph Smith's Translation of the Bible, A History and Commentary* (Provo, UT: Brigham Young University Press, 1975.)

4. D&C 44; compare Wood, 2[1833]:100-101, where it was

published as Chapter 46. For background, see Cook, *Revelations*, 62, 132.

5. This conference was held on June 3-6, 1831, and is discussed more fully below.

6. This has been a persistent concept among Mormons. It comes largely from the environment of Immediate Millennialism in which the church originated. Many Protestant churches in the United States in the nineteenth century—especially those arising as a consequence of the Second Great Awakening—believed that the Millennium was literally just a matter of days away (Marty E. Marty, *Pilgrims in Their Own Land: 500 years of Religion in America* [Boston: Little, Brown and Co., 1984], 185-208; Michael Barkun, *Crucible of the Millennium: The Burned-over District of New York in the 1840s* [Syracuse, NY: Syracuse University Press, 1986]; Ernest Lee Tuveson, *Redeemer Nation: The Idea of America's Millennial Role* [Chicago: University of Chicago Press, 1968]; Richard T. Hughes, ed., *The American Quest for the Primitive Church* [Urbana: University of Illinois Press, 1988]; Richard T. Hughes and C. Leonard Allen, *Illusions of Innocence: Protestant Primitivism in America, 1630-1875* [Chicago: University of Chicago Press, 1988]; and Nathan O. Hatch, *The Democratization of American Christianity* [New Haven, CT: Yale University Press, 1989]).

This attitude was reinforced by a number of revelations which made the Second Coming seem imminent (D&C 1; 2; 27:5-18; 29; 33; 35; 38; 39:16-24; 58; 88; 109; 110; 133). It is also evident in the thinking and writing of early church leaders (*HC*, 1:294-95, 439-40; 4:15, 401; 7:8; Thomas G. Alexander, *Things in Heaven and Earth: The Life and Times of Wilford Woodruff, a Mormon Prophet* [Salt Lake City: Signature Books, 1991], 320-21; Grant Underwood, "Seminal versus Sesquicentennial Saints: A Look at Mormon Millennialism," *Dialogue: A Journal of Mormon Thought* 14 [Spring 1981]: 32-44; "Millenarianism and the Early Mormon Mind," *Journal of Mormon History* 9 [1982]: 41-51; and "The Millenarian World of Early Mormonism," Ph.D. diss., University of California at Los Angeles, 1988).

Concerning this period, Orson Pratt later recalled:

> It was expected that when the Saints gathered to Jackson County, there would be a perfect paradise, and that there would be an end to trouble and to opposition. And when the Saints were driven out from Jackson County, almost all in the Church expected that they would speedily be restored; and a person was considered almost an apostate that would say, they would not come back in five years, or ten at the furthest; but the prevailing opinion seemed to be that it would take place immediately.
>
> When Zion's Camp went up, and found the Saints all scattered abroad, what did we hear? Why, all in camp were on the tiptoe to have Zion redeemed immediately; perhaps some would stretch their faith and put it off for five years; but those were considered weak in the faith. This was their extreme enthusiasm. . . .
>
> Again, take the subject of the coming of Christ, and as far back as 1831, I remember that I came on from New York to Kirtland, Ohio, and I found many Saints thinking that Christ would come immediately. . . . No doubt they felt exceedingly anxious to have him come, as we all do, and this anxiety overcame them, and hence they were mistaken (*JD* 3:17).

The expectations of immediacy have settled since the turn of the twentieth century. Although the Second Coming and related matters still remain a major doctrine of the Mormon church, and although apocryphal folktales still abound about its date and related topics, by and large the concept no longer occupies the attention of Latter-day Saints as it once did (see Thomas G. Alexander, *Mormonism in Transition* [Urbana: University of Illinois Press, 1986], 288-90).

7. D&C 45; compare Wood, 2[1835]:128-32, where this revelation was published as Section 15. For historical background, see Cook, *Revelations*, 63, 132.

At this point Whitmer switches from quoting the 1833 Book of Commandments to citing the 1835 Kirtland edition of the Doctrine and Covenants and relying on it almost exclusively for the remainder of his history. In addition, instead of copying the text of a revelation in full, he begins the practice of simply indicating the place where the text was later to be inserted.

8. Millennialists believed that natural disasters punished the ungodly and were tokens of the approaching Second Coming (Barkun, *Crucible of the Millennium*, 103-12). This attitude came into the early church with its first converts and was accepted as doctrine (see, for example, *HC*, 1:294-95, 439-40; 4:145, 401; 7:8; see also Grant Underwood, *The Millenarian World of Early Mormonism* [Urbana: University of Illinois Press, 1993]).

Chapter 4
Welcoming Unbelievers

CHAPTER IV

[p. 23] John Murdock[1] and others held a meeting in the city of Cleveland Ohio, in the Masonick hall by the request of some of the Citizens of said City. An opportunity which some sought to bring about their evil designs. Elder Murdock addressed the congregation on the subject of the gospel; and warned the inhabitants of that place to flee the wrath to come.

Others followed him and while they were yet speaking One of the congregation came towards the stand and kneeled down and began to pray, a sign to the bandity to begin their abuse, At this time they began to blow out the candles [and] throw inkstands and books &c at the speaker. and one of the brethren prayed that the Lord would stop the utterance of the fellow that came and kneeled at the stand and he became silent and could not rise from his knees for some time, because of the prayer of faith.

In the beginning of the church, while yet in her infancy, the disciples used to exclude unbelievers, which caused some to marvel, and converse about this matter because of the things that were written in the Book of Mormon. Therefore the Lord deigned to speak on this subject, that his people might come to understanding. and said, that he had always given to his Elders to conduct all meetings as they were led by the spirit. See Revelation Given March 1831. Book Doctrine and Covenants first edition printed at Kirtland Ohio. Page 132 Section 16. insert the Revelation.[2]

NOTES

1. John Murdock was born on July 15, 1792, in Kortright, Delaware County, New York. He moved to Cuyahoga County, Ohio, about 1820 and joined with Sidney Rigdon in the Campbellite movement about 1828. He married Julia Class on December 14, 1823; they had five children: Orrice, John Riggs, Phebe, Joseph, and Julia. He was baptized into the Mormon church by Parley P. Pratt on November 5, 1830, ordained an elder sometime that same month, and sent preaching numerous times in the Western Reserve. His wife Julia died April 30, 1831. Their children, Joseph and Julia, twins about eleven months old, were adopted by Joseph and Emma Smith.

Murdock was appointed to travel to Jackson County, Missouri, with Hyrum Smith in June 1831. On June 6 he was ordained a high priest. Returning to Ohio in June 1832, he was appointed in August to preach in the "eastern countries." He preached in the Kirtland area for seven months, from September to April, while attending the School of the Prophets, then left for New York with Zebedee Coltrin on April 3, 1833. They returned to Kirtland a little over a year later.

In 1834 Murdock joined with some 200 other brethren in Zion's Camp, the armed march to Missouri. On July 7 he was appointed a member of the Clay County high council, though he returned to Ohio, arriving in January 1835. He received his patriarchal blessing there on February 20 from Joseph Smith, Sr., and left for a mission to Delaware County, New York, March 5. He married Amoranda Turner on February 4, 1836, in New York and returned to Kirtland on February 24.

From Kirtland, he left for Missouri on June 3, arriving in Ray County in mid-July. He assisted in settling the town of Far West that same year. His wife Amoranda died in August 1837. Murdock then married Electa Allen on May 3, 1838. From this marriage came three children: Gideon, Rachel, and Hyrum Smith.

In June Murdock was appointed to settle in DeWitt, Missouri. However, he, along with the rest of the Saints, were expelled from the state the next year. The Murdock family settled near Lima, Illinois, where they resided until 1841. At that time they moved to Nauvoo. Murdock was ordained bishop of the Nauvoo Ward on August 20, 1842. He served until November 29, 1844, when he left on a mission to the Eastern States.

Murdock's wife Electa died on October 16, 1845. On March 13, 1846, he married Sarah Zuflet. This union produced two children: George Weire (adopted) and Brigham Young. Murdock and his family left for the West in May, arriving in the Salt Lake Valley the next year on September 24, 1847. Murdock became a member of the Salt Lake high council and was appointed bishop of the Salt Lake Fourteenth Ward in 1849. He served to January 1853. On April 9, 1854, Murdock was ordained a patriarch by Heber C. Kimball.

Murdock and his family resided in Lehi, Utah, from 1854 to the time they moved to Beaver, Utah, in 1867. He died on December 23, 1871 (Cook, *Revelations*, 80).

2. D&C 46; compare Wood, 2[1835]:132-34, for text. For background, see Cook, *Revelations*, 63-64, 132-33. As a consequence, non-Mormons were admitted to all public meetings of the church.

Chapter 5
Gathering to Ohio

CHAPTER. V.

The time drew near for the brethren from the State of New York to arrive at Kirtlan[d,] Ohio. And some had supposed that it was the place of gathering even the place of the New Jerusalem spoken of in the Book of Mormon according to the visions and revelations received in the last days. There was no preparation made for the reception of the Saints. from the east. The Bishop being anxious to know something concerning the matter. Therefore the Lord spoke unto Joseph Smith Jr. as follows[1]:

[p. 24] Thus saith the Lord, it is necessary that ye should remain for the present time in your place of abode as it shall be suitable to your circumstances. And inasmuch as ye have lands, ye shall impart to the eastern brethren. And inasmuch as ye have not lands, let them buy for the present time in those regions round about; as seemeth them good; for it must needs be necessary that they have places to live for [the] present time; It must needs be necessary that ye save all the money that ye can, and that ye obtain all that ye can, that in time ye may be enabled to purchase lands for inheritances: even the City[2]. The place is not yet to be revealed; but after your brethren come from the east, there are certain men to be appointed and to them <it> shall be given; to know the place, or to them it shall be revealed, and they shall be appointed, to purchase the lands and to make a commencement to lay the foundation of the City; and then ye shall begin to be gathered with your families, every man according to his family: according to his circumstances, and as is appointed to them by the Bishop and elders of the church according to the laws and commandments which ye have received: and which ye shall hereafter receive, and thus it is. Amen.

NOTES

1. D&C 48; compare Wood, 2[1835]:190-91, for text. For background, see Cook, *Revelations*, 65, 133.

2. It is important to note the difference between members of the church building a home for Joseph Smith and other church authorities and the "hireling priests" that Whitmer and other Mormons constantly preach against. Joseph was built a home as compensation for his time in attending to the financial business of the church and other day-to-day administrative work, not as compensation for preaching and teaching. "Hireling priests" were defined as those people hired by a congregation to preach to the members of the church. In American Protestant practice a body of congregation members determined the hiring and firing of the minister and also tended to administrative matters. At this time Joseph was doing both. Thus, in recognition of his time spent in administrative details, and in view of the fact that such business was taking away from the amount of time he had to look after and house his family, the Saints built Joseph a home as a partial remuneration. It should be remembered that in both

Missouri and in Nauvoo, Joseph owned and worked a farm to take care of the needs of his family.

Chapter 6
Becoming Scribe

CHAPTER VI

I returned from Nelson Ohio where I and Lyman Wight had built a branch of the Church of Christ.

I was appointed by the voice of the Elders to keep the Church record.[1] Joseph Smith Jr. said unto me You must also keep the Church history. I would rather not do it but observed that the will of the Lord be done, and if he desires it, I desire that he would manifest it through Joseph the Seer. And thus came the word of the Lord[2]:

Behold it is expedient in me that my servant John Whitmer should write and keep a regular history, and assist you my servant Joseph, in transcribing all things which shall be [p. 25] given you, until he is called to further duties. Again, verily I say unto you, that he can also lift up his voice in meetings when ever it shall be expedient.

And again, I say unto you, that it shall be appointed unto him to keep the church record and history continually, for Oliver Cowdery I have appointed unto another office. Wherefore, it shall be given him, inasmuch as he is faithful, by the

Comforter, to write these things: even so. Amen.

Oliver Cowdery has written the commencement of the church history, commencing at the time of the finding of the plates, up to June 12, 1831.[3]

From this date I have written the things that I have written, and they are a mere sketch of the things that have transpired, they are however all that seemed to me wisdom to write - many things happened that are to be lamented because of the weakness and instability of man. The Devil having a gr[e]at hold on the hearts of the children of men, and the foolish traditions of our fathers, is to be lamented, for they count themselves the children of wisdom, and great knowledge, in consequence of which, the fulness of the gosple finds its way to but few of the hearts of this generation. Although their hearts must be penetrated, whether they will hear or whether they will forbear.

Permit me here to remark, that David Whitmer,[4] Oliver Cowdery, and Martin Harris,[5] were the three Witnesses, whose names are attached to the Book of Mormon according to the prediction of the Book, who knew and seen, for a surety, into whose presence the angel of God came and showed them the Plates, the ball, the directors,[6] &c. And also other witnesses even eight Viz. Christian Whitmer,[7] Jacob Whitmer,[8] John Whitmer, Peter Whitmer Jr., Hyram Page,[9] Joseph Smith, [Sr.,][10] Hyram Smith,[11] and Samuel H. Smith[12] are the men to whom Joseph Smith Jr showed the Plates, these witnesses names go forth also of the truth of this work in the last days. To the convincing or condemning of this generation in the last day.[13]

[p. 26] Some of the brethren arrived from the State of New York, Samuel H. Smith & Orson Pratt, who were prospered on their journey. The disciples increased daily, and miricles were wrought such as healing the sick casting out devils, and the church grew and multiplied in numbers, grace, and knowledge.

Leman Copley[14] one of the disciples, who was formerly a shaker quaker,[15] he was anxious that some of the elders should go to his former brethren and preach the gospel. He also teased[16] to be ordained to preach himself, and desired that the Lord should direct in this and all matters & thus saith the Lord:

Given at Kirtland March 1831. Published in the first edition at Kirtland, page 191. insert the revelation.[17]

The above named brethren went and proclaimed according to the revelation given to them, but the shakers hearkened not to their words, and received not the gospel at that time; for they were bound up in tradition and priestcraft, and thus they are led away with foolish and vain imaginations.

For a perpetual memory, to the shame and confusion of the devil—permit me, to say a few things, respecting the proceedings of some of those who were disciples, and some remain among us, and will, and have come from under the error and enthusiam, which they had fallen.

Some had visions and could not tell what they saw. Some would fancy to themselves that they had the sword of Laban, and would wield it as expert as a light dragoon, some would act like an Indian in the act of scalping, some would slide or scoot ond the floor, with the rapidity of a serpent, which the[y] termed sailing in the boat to the Lamanites, preaching the gospel. And many other vain and foolish manoeuvers, that are unseeming, and unprofitable to mention. Thus the devil blinded the eyes of some good and honest disciples. I write these things to show how ignorant and undecerning children are [p. 27] and how easy man kind is lead as tray, notwithstanding the things of God that are written, concerning his Kingdom.

These things griev[e]d the servants of the Lord, and some

conversed together on this subject, and others came in and we were at Joseph Smith Jr. the Seers, and made it a matter of consultation, for many would not turn from their folly, unless God would give a revelation, therefore the Lord spoke to Joseph saying. Revelation given Kirtland May 1831. Printed at Kirtland first edition Page 134, Section 17. insert the Revelation.[18]

NOTES

1. Whitmer was officially called at a conference held on April 9, 1831 (*Far West Record*, 5; and Cook, *Revelations*, 64-65, 133).

2. D&C 47; compare Wood, 2[1835]:190 (Section 63), which was given in March 1831, and an additional revelation given the following November (Wood, 2[1835]:155 [Section 38]). For historical background, see Cook, *Revelations*, 64-65, 133.

After the conference called Whitmer to the position, he asked Joseph Smith for a revelation to confirm it instead of the other way around as shown in the documents.

3. The whereabouts of this manuscript is unknown. David Whitmer seems to have made passing reference to it in an 1884 interview (see Lyndon W. Cook, ed., *David Whitmer Interviews: A Restoration Witness* [Orem, UT: Grandin Book Co., 1991], 114). The manuscript apparently did exist, however, at one time, although who may have had it is uncertain (see Franklin D. Richards to George Schweich, 15 Oct. 1889, Franklin D. Richards Collection, archives, Historical Department, Church of Jesus Christ of Latter-day Saints, Salt Lake City, Utah (hereafter LDS archives); Andrew Jenson to Franklin D. Richards, 5 Sept. 1893, Richards Collection; Franklin D. Richards to Andrew Jenson, 9 Sept. 1893, Andrew Jenson Collection, LDS archives; Andrew Jenson to Franklin D. Richards, 14 Sept. 1893, Richards Collection).

4. David Whitmer was born on January 7, 1805, to Peter Whitmer and Mary Musselman near Harrisburg, Dauphin County, Pennsylvania. In 1829, he, in company with Oliver Cowdery and Martin Harris, became one of the Three Witnesses of the Book of Mormon. He was baptized in June 1829. On January 9, 1831, he married Julia Ann Jolly; they became the parents of two children. He was ordained an elder on April 6, 1830, and moved his family to Kirtland, Ohio, by June. Here he was ordained a high priest on October 25.

Whitmer and his family moved to Jackson County, Missouri, around October 1832. On July 7, 1834, he was chosen and ordained to be the successor of Joseph Smith and "president of the church in Zion" (Missouri). He left Missouri for Kirtland about September.

On February 14, 1835, Whitmer, Martin Harris, and Oliver Cowdery, along with Joseph Smith, in accordance with an earlier revelation (D&C 18:26-30, 37-40), met with the veterans of the paramilitary march on Missouri (Zion's Camp) and chose members for the original Quorum of the Twelve Apostles; on February 28 the four again met to fill the original First Quorum of the Seventy.

Whitmer remained in Kirtland to participate in the dedicatory services of the Kirtland temple in March 1836. In 1837, however, he allied himself with dissenters and returned to Missouri on July 29 bitterly disillusioned. He was rejected as president of the church in Zion at a conference held February 5, 1838, along with his two counselors, William W. Phelps and John Whitmer. David Whitmer was excommunicated on April 13, 1838, for apostasy. Following his excommunication, David and his family settled in Richmond, Ray County, Missouri, where he operated a livery stable. He was elected to fill an unexpired term of mayor in Richmond from 1867-68.

Whitmer never rejoined the LDS church, nor did he ever become a member of any other church. Throughout the remainder of his life, he constantly reaffirmed his faith in Joseph Smith and the Book of Mormon. He died on January 25, 1888, in

Richmond (Cook, *Revelations*, 24-25, 123; *LDSBE*, 1:263-71; Anderson, *Witnesses*, 67-92; see also Cook, *David Whitmer Interviews*, for a summary of Whitmer's recollections and testimony).

5. Martin Harris, a son of Nathan Harris and Rhoda Lapham, was born on May 18, 1783, in Easttown, Saratoga County, New York. He married his first cousin, Lucy Harris; they became the parents of three children. A prominent local landowner and farmer, Martin owned 240 acres in the Palmyra area.

In 1829 Harris served as a scribe to Joseph Smith during the dictation of the Book of Mormon; that June, along with David Whitmer and Oliver Cowdery, he became one of the Three Witnesses. Harris financed publication of the Book of Mormon in 1830.

Baptized on April 6, 1830, Harris was ordained a priest and on June 3, 1831, a high priest. He became a member of the Kirtland high council in February 1834. The following April he marched with Zion's Camp to Missouri.

On February 14, 1835, Harris, along with Oliver Cowdery, David Whitmer, and Joseph Smith, chose the first Quorum of the Twelve Apostles; on February 28 they filled the ranks of the First Quorum of the Seventy. Harris married Caroline Young in 1837, following the death of his first wife; they had five children. He was excommunicated that December and rebaptized on November 6, 1842.

Harris never made the move to Nauvoo, Illinois, nor did he initially follow Brigham Young after Joseph Smith was killed in 1844. Instead, he joined with James J. Strang, serving a mission to England in 1846. In January 1847 Harris and William E. McLellan joined together to organize a new church, the Church of Christ, in Kirtland, Ohio. This organization, however, lasted a few years before it eventually disintegrated.

Harris's wife, Caroline, left him in 1856 to gather with the Utah Saints. Martin finally followed in August 1870, where he was rebaptized and received his temple endowment the next month. He died on July 9, 1875, in Clarkston, Cache County, Utah (Cook, *Revelations*, 8-9, 121; *LDSBE*, 1:271-76; Steven L. Shields, *Divergent Paths of the Restoration*, 4th rev. ed. [Los Angeles, CA: Restoration Research, 1990], 49-50; and Anderson, *Witnesses*, 95-120).

6. The "ball" and "directors" mentioned here refer to the Liahona, which was given to Lehi to help guide his family in their journey through the desert in the Book of Mormon. (See I Ne. 16:10; Alma 37:38-40; D&C 17:1.)

7. Christian Whitmer, oldest son of Peter Whitmer, Sr., and Mary Musselman, was born on January 18, 1798, in Pennsylvania. While quite young, he moved with his parents from Pennsylvania to Seneca County, New York. Here he married Anne Schott on February 22, 1825, and established himself as a shoemaker. Christian and his wife were baptized in Seneca Lake on April 11, 1830, by Oliver Cowdery. By June, Christian had been ordained a teacher and an elder in 1831.

Whitmer and his wife moved to Ohio with the rest of the New York Saints in 1831; in 1832 the family resettled in Jackson County, Missouri. On September 15 he was called to preside over the elders in Jackson County and was ordained a high priest on August 21, 1833, by Simeon Carter.

In November the Whitmer family was driven out of Jackson County, losing their farm and most of their belongings. They settled temporarily in Clay County, where Whitmer was chosen to serve on the high council on July 3, 1834. He occupied this position until his death on November 27, 1835 (*LDSBE*, 1:276).

8. Jacob Whitmer, another of the Eight Witnesses of the Book of Mormon, was the second son of Peter Whitmer, Sr., and Mary Musselman. He was born in Pennsylvania on January 27, 1800. While still a boy, Jacob moved to New York with his older brother Christian and his parents. On September 29, 1825, he married his sister-in-law Elizabeth Schott; they had nine children.

Jacob and his wife were baptized in Seneca Lake on April 11, 1830. With the rest of the Whitmer family, they moved to Ohio in 1831 and subsequently settled in Jackson County, Missouri. With the rest of the church, they were expelled from the county late in 1833. Jacob moved his family to Clay and then to Caldwell County. While in Caldwell County, he acted as a temporary high councilor and also as a member of the building committee for the erection of the projected Far West temple.

Whitmer severed his connection with the LDS church in 1838 and moved to Richmond, Ray County, Missouri. He resided there until his death on April 21, 1856 (*LDSBE*, 1:276-77).

9. Hiram Page was born in Vermont in 1800. He studied medicine and traveled considerably throughout Canada and the state of New York, finally establishing his practice in Seneca County. There he became acquainted with the Whitmer family and married Catherine Whitmer, a sister of David, Christian, and John Whitmer, and daughter of Peter Whitmer, Sr., and Mary Musselman, on November 10, 1825; they had nine children.

Hiram and his wife were baptized by Oliver Cowdery in Seneca Lake on April 11, 1830. Shortly afterwards, Page came into possession of a "peepstone," or "seer stone," through which he received revelations which contradicted Joseph Smith. A number of church members believed in Page's revelations, including the Whitmer family and Oliver Cowdery. Joseph Smith was away from home at the time. A conference held in September 1830 investigated the matter and Page recanted.

The Page family moved to Kirtland in 1831 and settled in Missouri the following year. During the 1833 disturbances there, Page was selected, together with three others, to go to Lexington, Missouri, see the circuit court judge, and obtain a peace warrant. Upon receiving their affidavits, Judge John F. Ryland issued writs against some of the ringleaders and gave them to the Mormon delegation to return to the sheriff in Jackson County; these writs, however, accomplished little in warding off depredations.

Following the exodus from Jackson County, Page took an active part in the church in Clay County. In 1836 he became one of the founders of the town of Far West in Caldwell County, Missouri. In 1838 he severed his connection with the church and moved to Ray County, where he resided until his death on August 12, 1852 (*LDSBE*, 1:277-78).

10. Joseph Smith, Sr., the second son of Asahel Smith and Mary Duty, was born on July 12, 1771, in Topsfield, Essex County, Massachusetts. He moved to Tunbridge, Orange County, Vermont, in 1791 and assisted in clearing a large farm. On January 24, 1796, he married Lucy Mack; they had ten children, including church founder Joseph Smith.

In 1802 Smith rented his farm, engaged in the mercantile business, and later invested in a venture to ship and sell ginseng in China. He was swindled out of his profits by the shipmaster and sales agent and consequently sold his farm to pay his debts.

About 1815 Smith and shortly afterward his family moved to Palmyra, Wayne County, New York, where Smith later bought a farm and cleared 200 acres. The family lost this farm when they were unable to pay the last installment on the mortgage. From here, the Smiths moved to Manchester, Ontario County, New York, where they procured a home with sixteen acres of land. They lived here until they left with the rest of the Saints for Kirtland, Ohio, in 1831.

Smith was baptized on April 6, 1830. The following August, in company with his son Don Carlos, he filled a short mission to St. Lawrence County, New York, distributing a few copies of the Book of Mormon and visiting with and teaching his relatives. This mission resulted in the conversion of the entire family except for his brother Jesse and sister Susan.

Smith was ordained to the high priesthood on June 3, 1831, by Lyman Wight. On December 18, 1833, he was ordained a patriarch and president of the high priesthood under the hands of Joseph Smith, Jr., Oliver Cowdery, Sidney Rigdon, and Frederick G. Williams; on February 17, 1834, he was called as a member of the first standing Kirtland high council.

In 1836 Smith was sent on a mission with his brother John. They traveled over 2,400 miles, covering the states of Ohio, New York, Pennsylvania, Vermont, and New Hampshire. They visited the branches of the church, bestowed patriarchal blessings, preached, and baptized.

During the financial panic in Kirtland in 1837, Smith was sent to jail for debts. After his release in 1838, he moved to Far West, Missouri, arriving late that summer. Following the arrest of his sons in October 1838, Smith left Missouri for Quincy, Illinois, with his wife Lucy and their youngest children. The family settled in Nauvoo in the spring of 1839. Smith died of tuberculosis on September 14, 1840, in Nauvoo, Illinois (*LDSBE*, 1:181-82).

11. Hyrum Smith, a son of Joseph Smith, Sr., and Lucy Mack Smith, was born on February 9, 1800, in Tunbridge, Vermont. He was an older brother of church founder Joseph Smith. When Hyrum was about nineteen years old, the family moved to western New York. On November 2, 1826, he married Jerusha Barden in Manchester, New York; they had six children. Jerusha died on October 13, 1837. Later that year Smith married Mary Fielding; they had two children.

Smith was baptized in Seneca Lake sometime in June 1829. In a conference of the church in Far West, Missouri, on November 7, 1837, he was called as second counselor in the First Presidency following a vote which rejected Frederick G. Williams. On January 19, 1841, he was called to the office of patriarch over the whole church, succeeding his father, who had just died.

Hyrum and his brother Joseph were arrested together in Far West, Missouri, in October 1838, spent the winter together in Liberty Jail, and six years later died together at the hands of a mob while incarcerated in Carthage Jail, Illinois, on June 27, 1844 (*LDSBE*, 1:52-53).

For a summary of the conflicts which led up to the incarceration of Joseph and Hyrum in Carthage on charges of treason against the State of Illinois, see Edwin Brown Firmage and Richard Collin Mangrum, *Zion in the Courts* (Urbana: University of Illinois Press, 1988), 80-120.

12. Samuel H. Smith was born March 13, 1808, in Tunbridge, Orange County, Vermont, to Joseph Smith, Sr., and Lucy Mack Smith; he was a younger brother of the prophet Joseph Smith. Baptized on May 25, 1829, he became one of the Eight Witnesses to the Book of Mormon the following June. He was ordained an elder on June 9, 1830, and immediately sent on a six-month mission. He was sent on another mission to Kirtland, Ohio, with Orson Pratt, in February 1831. On June 3 he was ordained a high priest. He served a number of subsequent proselyting missions in the Midwest and eastern states.

In Kirtland Smith attended the School of the Prophets and assisted in laying the foundation stones for the Kirtland temple in July 1833. He moved to Far West, Missouri, in March 1838, and later settled at Marrowbone in Daviess County. A participant in the Battle of Crooked River in October 1838, Smith was forced from Missouri with the rest of the Saints in 1839. He moved to Quincy, Illinois, later moving onto George Miller's farm at Macomb. In 1840 Smith moved to Nauvoo. In January 1841, he was called to the presiding bishopric of the church and served as bishop of the Nauvoo Ward. He occupied a number of civil positions as well, being elected an alderman of the City of Nauvoo in February 1841 and serving as a member of the Nauvoo Legion.

Smith married Mary Bailey on August 13, 1834; they became the parents of four children; Mary died on January 25, 1841. Smith married Levira Clark of Geneva, Illinois, on May 3, 1841; they had three children. The family moved to Plymouth, Illinois, in the fall of 1842. Smith received his endowment on December 17, 1843. He died on July 30, 1844, in Nauvoo (Cook, *Revelations*, 34; *LDSBE*, 1:278-82).

13. For further information on the Eight Witnesses, see Anderson, *Witnesses*, 123-49.

14. Leman Copley was born in Connecticut in 1781. By 1800 the Copley family had moved to Pitsford, Vermont, where they joined the United Society of Believers in Christ's Second Coming, more popularly known as the Shaking Quakers, or Shakers. Leman moved to the Cleveland, Ohio, area—then the site of a large Shaker community—around 1820. He married "Salley" sometime during this period, and they had one child, Reuben.

By 1830 Leman held title to large tracts of land in Thompson, Ohio. He was baptized into the Mormon church and ordained an elder sometime around March 1831 and was appointed to accompany Sidney Rigdon and Parley P. Pratt in preaching the gospel to the Shaker community in Union Village, Ohio, near the Cleveland area, a mission which failed when the Shakers rejected the missionaries' message.

Copley originally agreed to permit members of the church emigrating from New York to settle on his property. By June 1831 he had changed his mind. This situation prompted the Saints of the Colesville, New York, Branch, which had settled on Copley's land, to move on to Missouri.

Fellowship in the church was withdrawn from Copley sometime during the summer of 1831 but was extended again sometime before October 1832. He testified against Joseph Smith during Philastus Hurlbut's trial before the Kirtland high council and was subsequently disfellowshipped. Again, he repented and was returned to full fellowship, this time on April 1, 1836.

Copley did not gather again with the Saints when they left the Ohio area. He became a successful farmer, with real estate valued at $3,500 in 1850. He died in Madison Township, Lake County, Ohio, sometime after 1860 (Cook, *Revelations*, 133-34).

For information on the Shakers, see Sydney E. Ahlstrom, *A Religious History of the American People* (New Haven: Yale University Press, 1972), 492-94; Lawrence Foster, *Religion and Sexuality* (Urbana: University of Illinois Press, 1984), 21-71; and Stephen J. Stein, *The Shaker Experience in America* (New Haven, CT: Yale University Press, 1992).

15. The United Society of Believers in Christ's Second Coming (the Millennial Church)—otherwise known as the Shaking Quakers, or "Shakers"—came to the United States from England. It was founded by Ann Lee Stanley, who immigrated with eight followers in 1774. Mother Ann Lee was the daughter of a Manchester blacksmith. Unschooled and illiterate, she was converted to the Shaking Quakers by Jane and James Wardley, leaders of the sect.

Lee apparently outshone all of the other members of the sect in the intensity of her piety. Her trances and visions convinced others and then herself that Christ's second coming would be in the form of a woman, and that she was that woman. She also became convinced that sexual relations were the root of all sin; this idea led to the practice of celibacy of the Shakers in America.

Lee and her small group of believers formed a somewhat radical group within the British Shaker body. Few people in England were persuaded by their noisy worship practices and the irrepressible preachers which she now led. Mistreatment, mob action, and imprisonment seemed to be their lot and only expectation; thus they emigrated to the United States, settling near Albany, New York. Poverty forced the group to establish a Christian communal living arrangement, something which had not previously been part of their message.

Upon Lee's death in 1784, capable leaders took the reins of leadership of the group and impressive gains were made. Converts were brought in and additional communities were established in New York, Massachusetts, Kentucky, and Ohio; it was in Ohio where the Mormons encountered them for the first time. A few converts to the LDS church were made, but the Shakers largely rejected the Mormon message.

The Shakers prospered through most of the nineteenth century; however, industrialization trends in post-Civil War America and the demands of factory life made communal living arrangements unfeasible. These developments disrupted the communities and caused the eventual disintegration of the sect (Ahlstrom, *A Religious History of the American People*, 492-94;

Lawrence Foster, *Religion and Sexuality, 21-71;* and *Women, Family, and Utopia: Communal Experiments of the Shakers, the Oneida Community, and the Mormons* [Syracuse, NY: Syracuse University Press, 1991],17-71).

16. In nineteenth-century usage, to "tease" meant to annoy or pester someone to get them to do something or change their mind about something.

17. D&C 49. This revelation was published as Section 65 in the 1835 edition. For the text, see Wood, 2[1835]:191-192; for background, see Cook, *Revelations,* 66-67, 133-34.

18. D&C 50; compare Wood, 2[1835]:134-36. This section discusses how to discern the presence of the spirit of the Lord from other influences. Properly differentiating spiritual impulses and manifestations for members of the church at this time was a problem. See Cook, *Revelations,* 67-69, 134.

Chapter 7
The High Priesthood

CHAPTER VII.

About these days the disciples arrived from State of New York. To this place Kirtland State of Ohio. They had some dificulty because of some that did not continue faithful, who denied the truth and turned unto fables.

June 3, 1831. A general conference was called, and a blessing promised, if the elders were faithful, and humble before him.[1] Therefore the elders assembled from the East, and the West, from the North and the South. And also many members.

Conference was opened by prayer and exortation by Joseph Smith Jr. the Revelator. After the business of the church was attended to according to the Covenants. The Lord made manifest to Joseph that it was necessary that such of the elders as were considered worthy, should be ordained to the high priesthood.[2]

The spirit of the Lord fell upon Joseph in an unusual manner. And prophecied that John the Revelator was then among the ten tribes of Israel who had been lead away by

Salmanaser King of israel, to prepare them for their return, from their Long dispersion, to again possess the land of their fathers. He prophecied many more things ~~that~~ [asking] ~~the many, he said that if Joseph Wakefield~~[3] [p. 28] that I have not written. After he had prophecied, he laid his hands upon Lyman Wight[4] to the High Priesthood after the holy order of God. And the Spirit [blank space] fell upon Lyman, and he prophecied, concerning the coming of Christ, he said that there were some in this congregation that should live until the Savior shoud decend from heaven, with a Shout, with all the holy angels with him. He said the coming of the Savior should be, like, the Sun rising in the east, and will cover the whole earth, so will the coming of the Son of man be. Yea, he will appear in his brightness, and consume all before him. And the hills will be laid low, and valies be exalted; and the crooked be made straight; and the rough Smooth. And some of my brethren Shall suffer marterdom, for the sake of the religion of Jesus Christ and seal the testimony of Jesus with their blood. He saw the hevans opened, and the Son of man sitting on the right hand of the Father. Making intercession for his brethren. the Saints. He said that God would work a work in these last days that tongue cannot express, and the mind ~~of~~ is not capable to conceive. The glory of the Lord shone around.

At this conferen[c]e these were ordained to the high priesthood, namely Lyman White [Wight], Sidney Rigdon, John Murdock[,] Reynolds Cahoon,[5] Harv[e]y Whitlock,[6] and Hyram Smith were ordained by ~~Lyman Whight exce[p]t S~~ Joseph Smith Jr except Sidney Rigdon.

The following by Lyman Whight by commandment. Parley P. Pratt, Thomas B. Marsh, Isaac Morly,[7] Edward Partridge[,] Joseph Wakefield,[8] Ezra Thayer, Martin Harris, Ezra Booth[9] who denied the faith[,] Harvy Whitlock denied the faith, also Joseph Wakefield, Joseph Smith Sen.[,] Joseph Smith Jr.[,] John Whitmer.

The Bishop then proceeded and blessed the above named and others by the laying on of hands. Isaac Morly and John Corrill[10] were ordained as bishops counsellors to Edward Partridge

Joseph Smith Jr. Prophecied the day Previous that the [p. 29] man of Sin should be revealed. While the Lord poured out his spirit upon his servants, the Devil took occation, to make known his power, he bound Harvy Whitlock <and John Murdock> so that he could not speak and others were affected but the Lord showed to Joseph the Seer the design of this thing, he commanded the devil in the name of Christ and he departed to our joy and comfort. ~~Also~~

Therefore a part of the Revelation given at Fayette New York was fulfilled. The churches of the State of New York had moved to Ohio, with their Wives and their children, and all their Substance some purchased farms others rented, and thus they situated themselves as convenient as they could. The day being now far spent and the conference was adjourned.

NOTES

1. This conference lasted from June 3-6, 1831. Ordinations to the "High Priesthood," or office of high priest, were made for the first time. John Corrill and Isaac Morley were ordained "assistants," or counselors, to Bishop Edward Partridge (*Far West Record*, 6-9; *HC*, 1:157, 175-81).

2. This refers to the office of high priest in the Melchizedek priesthood, not to the Melchizedek priesthood as a whole (Cook, *Revelations*, 71-83, 136-37n6).

3. No mention is made in the minutes of the meeting of any particular comments to Joseph Wakefield at this time. For further information on Wakefield, see n. 8 below.

4. Lyman Wight was born on May 9, 1796, in Fairfield, Herkimer County, New York. On January 5, 1823, he married Harriett Benton in Henrietta, New York; they had six children. The family moved to Warrensville, Ohio, about 1826 and remained there until 1830. In May 1829 the Wight family joined Sidney Rigdon in the Campbellite movement and entered into a covenant of "common stock"—a communal arrangement based on New Testament teachings—with Isaac Morley, Titus Billings, and others.

In February 1830 Wight moved to Kirtland. He and his family were baptized into the Mormon church that November. He was ordained an elder on November 20 and a high priest on June 3, 1831. Also in June he was appointed to travel to Missouri with John Corrill. They arrived in Jackson County on August 12. Wight was called to preside over Branch Number Seven on September 11, 1833. After the expulsion of the Saints from the county a month and a half later, Wight settled his family in Clay County.

On January 1, 1834, Wight travelled with Parley P. Pratt to Kirtland, Ohio, to counsel with church leaders about regaining the Saints' lands in Jackson County. The pair arrived about February 22. Wight travelled with Pratt, Joseph Smith, Sidney Rigdon, and others through Pennsylvania and New York to recruit for Zion's Camp and the pending march to Missouri.

Following the dissolution of Zion's Camp on June 22, Wight was called to the Clay County high council. On March 13, 1835, he left on a mission to Cincinnati and returned to Clay County on May 18. On November 3 he left for Kirtland again, this time to participate in the construction of the temple and to attend the School of the Prophets. Following dedication of the temple in March 1836, he left again for Missouri, arriving in early May.

In February 1837 Wight relocated his family in Caldwell

County, Missouri, and to the town of Adam-Ondi-Ahman on February 1, 1838. He was appointed counselor in the Adam-Ondi-Ahman Stake presidency on June 28, 1838. Wight was arrested on murder and treason charges in November 1838 during the "Mormon War" and incarcerated from November until April 1839 in Liberty Jail, along with Joseph Smith and others. Along with Smith and his fellow prisoners, Wight escaped during a prison transfer on April 19, 1839, and joined the rest of the Saints in Quincy, Illinois, a couple of months later. Five years after this relocation, Wight was appointed to the secret Mormon political caucus called the Council of Fifty. He began attending meetings on May 3, 1844, and received his endowment in the Nauvoo temple on May 14.

In accordance with the Council of Fifty's decisions of 1844-45, Wight prepared a group to move to Texas in the spring of 1845. The colony arrived sometime late in July. They spent the first winter at an evacuated fort called Georgetown in Williamson County, Texas. In April 1846, the group moved south to a point on the Colorado River four miles north of Austin. During the summer of 1846 the colony relocated to an area called Zodiac, four miles south of Fredericksburg, Gillespie County, Texas, on the Perdinales River.

Wight married his first plural wife, Mary Hawley, in 1845; they had two children. He also married Mary Ann Otis, had three children, and married Margaret Ballentine, producing one child. A member of the Quorum of the Twelve Apostles since 1841, Wight was excommunicated on December 3, 1848, because of a pamphlet he published rejecting Brigham Young's leadership.

In 1851, after floods destroyed the Zodiac colony, its members moved to Hamilton's Creek, about eight miles south of Burnet. In 1853, they moved again, this time to a site on the Medina River, twelve miles south of Bandera, Texas. The new location was named Mountain Valley. Wight died on March 31, 1858, in Dexter, Medina County, Texas, about eight miles from San Antonio. He was buried back at the old colonial site of Zodiac (Cook, *Revelations*, 82-83, 139-140; *LDSBE*, 1:93-96;

Steven L. Shields, *Divergent Paths of the Restoration* 4th rev. ed. [Los Angeles, CA: Restoration Research, 1990], 46-48).

    5. Reynolds Cahoon, a son of William Cahoon and Mehitabel Hodge, was born on April 30, 1790, in Cambridge, Washington County, New York. He married Thirza Stiles on December 11, 1810; they had seven children. The family moved to the Ohio region in 1811 where Reynolds began farming. A year later Reynolds enlisted to fight against the British in the War of 1812.

    In 1825 Cahoon moved his family near Kirtland, Ohio. He was baptized on October 11, 1830, by Parley P. Pratt and, shortly after his baptism, was ordained an elder by Sidney Rigdon. On June 3, 1831, he was ordained a high priest by Joseph Smith. Later that month he was appointed to travel to Jackson County, Missouri, with Samuel H. Smith; Cahoon was back in Kirtland by the following September. On October 11, 1831, he was called to obtain money and/or property to assist in finishing the revision of the Bible.

    On February 10, 1831, Cahoon was ordained a counselor to Bishop Newel K. Whitney. On May 4, 1833, he was appointed to obtain money to build "sacred edifices" in Kirtland. Cahoon was a charter member of the Kirtland Safety Society Anti-Banking Corporation in 1837.

    The Cahoon family moved to Missouri the next year, arriving on June 7. He was appointed a counselor in the stake presidency of Adam-Ondi-Ahman on June 28. When Mormons were forced from the state toward the end of that year, the Cahoons settled in Iowa. Cahoon was called as a counselor in the Iowa Stake presidency on October 19, 1839.

    Four years later, on October 12, 1843, Cahoon received his Nauvoo temple endowment. He became a member of the Council of Fifty on March 11, 1844. On January 24, 1845, he received his patriarchal blessing from John Smith. He was married ("sealed") to Lucina Roberts Johnson on January 16, 1846; they had three children. That same day he was also sealed to Mary

Hildrath; they had no children.

Cahoon relocated to Winter Quarters in 1846, following the exodus from Nauvoo, arriving in Salt Lake City, Utah, on September 23, 1848. He died in the South Cottonwood Ward, Salt Lake County, Utah, on April 29, 1861 (Cook, *Revelations*, 73, 138).

6. Harvey G. Whitlock was born in 1809 in Massachusetts. By 1830 he was married to a woman named Minerva; they had eight children. He was baptized and ordained an elder before June 3, 1831, when he was ordained a high priest by Joseph Smith. Later that month, he was appointed to travel to Jackson County, Missouri, with David Whitmer. Whitlock then moved his family to Missouri and resided in the Whitmer Branch. Along with the rest of the Saints, they were expelled from the county in late 1833.

Whitlock was stripped of his membership in the church in 1835. A revelation given November 16, 1835, counseled him to forsake his sins, live righteously, and go immediately to Kirtland. On January 30, 1836, a conference held by the First Presidency authorized his rebaptism and reordination as a high priest.

Whitlock officially withdrew from the church in 1838 during the Missouri civil war. By 1840 the family was residing in Cedar County, Iowa, but by 1850 they had moved to Salt Lake City, where Whitlock practiced medicine. In February 1851 Whitlock was arrested as an accessory to theft. He was rebaptized about 1858. He moved his family again, this time to California, arriving sometime around 1864. While there, he joined the Reorganized LDS church. The date of his death is not known (Cook, *Revelations*, 81, 139).

7. Isaac Morley was born on March 11, 1786, in Montague, Hampshire County, Massachusetts. On June 20, 1812, he married Lucy Gunn in Massachusetts; they had seven children.

The Morleys moved to the Ohio region sometime before 1830, where Isaac assisted in introducing the scientific study and application of experimental results in crop production into the area. They were baptized on November 15, 1830, and Isaac was ordained an elder shortly afterwards. On June 3, 1831, he was ordained a high priest and set apart as an "assistant," or counselor, to Bishop Edward Partridge.

Morley was called to travel to Missouri with Ezra Booth later that month. The pair arrived sometime in July. On September 11, about the same time Ezra Booth denounced Mormonism, Morley was chastised for unbelief and directed to sell his farm in Kirtland and relocate in Jackson County. The family did so, becoming members of the Independence Branch. They were expelled with the rest of the Saints in late 1833 and moved into Clay County.

On June 23, 1834, Morley was called to return to Kirtland to participate in the ordinances of washing and anointing. He left for Kirtland early in 1835 and arrived sometime before May. Shortly after arriving, Morley was called to accompany Edward Partridge on a mission to the Eastern States. They left Kirtland on June 2 and returned late the following October, when Morley was called to attend Hebrew school and the upcoming solemn assembly. Morley returned to Missouri mid-1836. That fall the family moved to Far West, Caldwell County, Missouri, and on November 7, 1837, was ordained a patriarch.

Morley was arrested in November 1838 and jailed on charges of treason, arson, and murder, though not convicted. The family, with the rest of the Saints, left the state during the winter of 1838-39, settling in Yelrome (Morley spelled backwards), Hancock County, Illinois, in 1839. Morley was a cooper by trade.

On October 22, 1840, Morley was called as president of the Lima Stake. After the stake was dissolved almost three years later, on June 11, 1843, he was called as president of the Lima Branch. He received his endowment on December 23. After moving to Nauvoo in 1845, he was sealed to Harriet Lenora Snow in 1846; they had no children. On January 14, 1846, he was sealed to Hannah Blakesley; they had three children. The family left Nauvoo in 1847 and moved on to Winter Quarters, where they remained until 1848. That year they emigrated to Utah.

Morley was called to be a member of the Salt Lake high council on February 15, 1849. The family helped settle Sanpete Valley later that year. Morley became a member of the general assembly of the Provisional State of Deseret and a member of the Utah Territorial Legislative Assembly, serving in the latter body from 1851-55. He died on June 24, 1865, in Fairview, Sanpete County, Utah (Cook, *Revelations*, 79-80, 139; *LDSBE*, 1:235-36).

8. Joseph Wakefield was born about 1792. He lived in Watertown, Jefferson County, New York, from 1820-33. Sometime before May 1831, he was baptized and ordained an elder. That same month he was called to preach with Parley P. Pratt in the Ohio region. On June 3 Wakefield was ordained a high priest and, later that month, was called to preach the gospel with Solomon Humphrey in the eastern states. The pair traveled to St. Lawrence County, New York, where they baptized future apostle George A. Smith in September 1832.

Wakefield is listed as owning property in Watertown in 1833. That summer he moved to Kirtland, Ohio, but soon became influenced by dissident Mormons. He joined a committee of Kirtland citizens who attempted to prove the Book of Mormon had been written by Solomon Spaulding. By January 1834 he had been excommunicated. Nothing is known of his subsequent life (Cook, *Revelations*, 69, 134).

9. Ezra Booth was born in Connecticut in 1792. By 1819 he had settled in Nelson, Ohio, where he married Dorcas Taylor on March 10. He became a Methodist minister. He converted to the Mormon church about May 1831, was ordained an elder later that month, and was ordained a high priest on June 3 by Lyman Wight.

Later in June Booth was appointed to travel to Missouri with Isaac Morley. They attended the August 4 conference in Jackson County in which the "land of Zion" was consecrated and set apart for the gathering of the Saints. Following the conference Booth was directed to purchase canoes for the elders returning to Ohio. He arrived about September 1.

Booth returned to Missouri later in the month on a mission. While there he lost faith in Joseph Smith, and his fellowship was withdrawn on September 6. He was chastised on September 11 for "evil actions." The next day he formally denounced Mormonism and started writing nine letters against the church, which were published in the *Ohio Star* from October through December 1831. In 1836 he attempted to establish his own church, the Church of Christ.

Booth was listed as residing in Mantua, Portage County, Ohio, in the 1860 census, where he owned a farm. The date of his death is not known (Cook, *Revelations*, 72-73, 138; Shields, *Divergent Paths of the Restoration*, 249).

10. John Corrill was born on September 17, 1794, in Worcester County, Massachusetts. By 1830 he had relocated to Ashtabula, Ohio, where he married a woman named Margaret; they had five children. Corrill was baptized on January 10, 1831, and ordained an elder sometime before June. He was ordained a high priest and set apart as an "assistant," or counselor, to Bishop Edward Partridge on June 3.

Corrill was appointed to travel with Lyman Wight to Jackson County in June 1831, and he moved his family to Missouri that same year. Corrill was then called to serve as branch president of Branch Number Four in Independence, Missouri.

He rose to prominence during the Missouri period (1831-38), frequently appointed to serve on committees and to act as an intermediary with antagonists and with the state militia. Many of the documents dealing with his work are copied here by John Whitmer. Corrill was jailed for a short time in Independence in 1833 and then was forced out of Jackson County with his family late that year, losing almost all of his property. Following the expulsion, the Corrills settled in Clay County, Missouri, where they bought some property.

On June 23, 1834, Corrill was called to travel to Kirtland and receive his "endowment." He participated in the temple dedication in March 1836 and was back in Clay County, Missouri the following November. Shortly afterwards he became one of the original settlers of the Mormon town of Far West in Caldwell County.

Corrill served in other capacities. On November 7, 1837, he was appointed "Keeper of the Lord's Storehouse" and on April 8, 1838, became Assistant Church Historian. In 1838 he was also elected as a state representative for Caldwell County.

Corrill first voiced his opposition to Joseph Smith in August 1838. On March 17, 1839, he was excommunicated. Later that year he published his short work, *A Brief History of the Church of Christ of Latter Day Saints (Commonly Called Mormons)*, in St. Louis. By 1840 Corrill was living in Quincy, Illinois. The date of his death is not known (Cook, *Revelations*, 68-69, 134; and *LDSBE*, 1:241-42).

Chapter 8
A Change of Venue

CHAPTER VIII.

June 6, 1831. Received a Revelation what to do. Printed at Kirtland Ohio, first edition Book Doctrine and Covenants Page 192. insert the revelation.[1]

After this revelation was received those elders were making all possible speed who were called to go according to commandment to fill their missions in their several courses.

At this time the Church at Thompson Ohio was involved in difficulty, becaus of the rebellion of Leman Copley.[2] Who would not do as he had previously agreed. Which thing confused the whole church and finally the Lord spake unto Joseph Smith Jr. the prophit saying[3]:

"Behold thus saith the Lord, even Alpha and Omega, the beginning and end, even he who was crucified for the sins of the world. Behold verily, verily I say unto you, my Servant Newel Knight,[4] You shall stand fast in the office wherewith you have been appointed; and if your brethren desire to escape their enemies, let them repent of all their sins; and become truly humble before me and contrite: and as the covenant which they made unto me, has been broken, even so it has [p. 30] become void and of none affect; and wo to him by whom this offenc cometh, for it had been better for him that he had been drowned in the depth of the sea; but blessed are they who have kept the covenant, and observed the commandment, for they shall obtain mercy.

Wherefore, go to now and flee the land lest your enemies come upon you; and take your journey ~~into the regions westward~~, and appoint whom you will to be your leader, and to pay moneys for you. And thus you shall take your Journey <into the regions> westward, unto the land of Missouri[5]; unto the borders of the Lamanites And after you have done Journeying, behold I say unto you, seek ye a living like unto men, until I prepare a place for you.

And again, be patient in tribulation until I come: and behold I come quickly, and my reward is with me, and they who have sought me early, shall find rest to their souls; even so: Amen.

After ~~some time~~ some of the elders had left and the time [came] for Joseph Smith Jr. and others to leave. Some of those who had been commanded to take their Journey speedily, [found] that some had denied the faith, and turned from the truth. And the church at Thompson Ohio, had not done according to the will of the [Lord]. Therefore, before Joseph and his company left thus came the word of the Lord; saying: Hearken O ye my people which profes my name, &c. See, book doctrine & covenants first edition published at Kirtland Ohio, page 197. Insert the revelation.[6]

The Church at Thompson made all possible haste to leave for Missouri, and left and none of their enemies harmed them.

The Church at Chardon Ohio was also anxious to take their journey to Missouri: and by much teasing they obtained a permit to take their journey.

NOTES

1. D&C 52; see Wood, 2[1835]:192-95, where it was published as Section 66. For background, see Cook, *Revelations*, 71-83, 135-40.

2. When the Colesville Branch arrived in the Kirtland area in May 1831, members were instructed to settle on some property in Thompson, Ohio, about sixteen miles northeast of Kirtland. The land was owned by Leman Copley, a recent convert to the church. However, with the attempt to initiate the law of consecration a few months later, where all property would be dedicated to the Lord and ownership turned over to the bishop, Copley rebelled and left the church. He also ordered the Colesville Saints off his property. As a consequence, they emigrated to Missouri. See Backman, *Heavens*, 44-47, 66.

3. D&C 54; compare Wood, 2[1835]:195-196. This revelation was printed here as Section 67. For background, see Cook, *Revelations*, 85, 140.

4. According to Pratt, at this time Newel Knight was the president of the Colesville Branch (Pratt, *Autobiography*, 54). Consequently, the revelation was given to him as a representative of the branch for the branch as a whole. After receiving the revelation, it was his responsibility as president to return to the branch and present it to the membership as a whole.

5. Missouri was identified as Zion in D&C 57:1-3.

6. D&C 56; compare Wood, 2[1835]:197-198, where the text appears as Section 69. For background, see Cook, *Revelations*, 88-91, 141.

Chapter 9
The Land of Zion

[P. 31] CHAPTER IX

There was much trouble and unbelief among those who call themselves disciples of Christ: Some apostatized, and became enemies to the cause of God, and percecuted the saints.

Now after the elders that were commanded to go to Missouri had arrived, they held a conference upon that land according to Revelation given in a preceeding commandment.[1]

And thus they rejoiced together upon the land of Zion And offered their Sacraments and oblations unto the Lord, for his mercy and goodness which endureth for ever.

When they had held their sacrament meetings, and the laying of the foundation of the City, and cornerstone of the Temple, the Lord gave commandments to return [to Kirtland].[2]

I hereby give a copy of the proceedings of the laying of the first logs of the City of Zion. As written by Oliver Cowdery.[3]

"After many struggles and afflictions, being persecuted by our enemies, we received inteligence by letter from our brethren, who were at the East. That br[others] Joseph and Sidney, and many others elders, were commanded to take their journey to this land, the Land of Missouri. Which was promised unto us should be the land of the inheritance of the Saints, and the place of the gathering in these last days. Which inteligenc cheered our hearts, and caused us to rejoice exceedingly. And by the special ~~direction~~ protection of the Lord, br Joseph Smith Jr. and Sidney Rigdon, in company with eight other elders, with the church from Colesville New York, consisting of about sixty souls, arivd in the month of July and by Revelation the place was made known where the Temple shall stand, and the City should commence. And by commandment twelve of us assembled ourselves together Viz. Elder Joseph Smith Jr. the Seer, Oliver Cowdery, Sidney Rigdon, Newel Knight,[4] William W. Phelps,[5] and Ezra Booth who denied the faith.

On the second day of August 1831, Brother Sidny [p. 32] Rigdon stood up and asked saying: Do you receive this land for the land of your inheritance with thankful hearts from the Lord? answer from all we do, Do you pledge yourselves to keep the laws of God on this land, which you have never have kept in your own land? We do. Do you pledge yourselves to see that others of your brethren, who shall come hither do keep the laws of God? We do. After prayer he arose and said, I now pronounce this land consecrated and dedicated to the Lord for a possession and inheritance for the Saints, (in the name of Jesus Christ having authority from him.) And for all the faithful Servants of the Lord to the rimotest ages of time Aamen.

The day following eight Elders viz. Joseph Smith Jr., Oliver Cowdery, Sidney Rigdon, Peter Whitmer Jr., Frederick G. Williams,[6] Wm. W. Phelps, Martin Harris, and Joseph Coe.[7] assembled together where the temple is to be erected. Sidney Rigdon dedicated the ground where the city is to Stand: and Joseph Smith Jr. laid a stone at the North east corner of the contemplated *Temple* in the name of the Lord Jesus of Nazareth. After all present had rendered thanks to the great ruler of the universe. Sidney Rigdon pronounced this Spot of ground wholy dedicated unto the Lord forever: Amen.[8]

Some of the Elders who travelled to the land of Missouri and preached by the way tarried here in this land, among whom is the Bishop E[dward] Partridge[,] Isaac Morley[,] and John Corrill. Some were sick on their way to this land but all were restored to health[.] among those who were sick was John Murdock Parley P. Pratt and Thomas B. Marsh—They all tarried until after they attended a conference in this land. They have since all gone to preach [p. 33] the gospel and call sinners to repentance.

There were some churches built by the way as they journeyed to this land (Mo.) and the people were warned of the danger they were in, if they did not repent.

And now when the Elders had returned to their homes in Ohio,[9] the churches needed much exortation in the absence of the Elders[.] many apostitized: but many have returned again to ~~from~~ the fold from whence they have strayed—And many mighty miracles were wrought by the Elders—one in particular which I shall here notice—which was wrought by Elders Emer[10] Harris Joseph Bracke[r]berry[11] and Wheeler Baldwin.[12] [This] Is [an incident regarding] an infirmity in an old lady who had been helpless for the space of eight years confined to her bed. she did not belong to this church but sent her request to the Elders who immediately attended to her call, and after their arrival praid [prayed] for her and laid their hands on her, and she was immediately made whole and magnified and praised God. and is now enjoying perfect health[.]

And thus the churches again prospered and the work of the Lord spread[.]

Shortly after Joseph Smith Jr[,] Oliver Cowdery[,] and Sidney Rigdon Returned [to Ohio] Sidney wrote a discription and an epistle according to commandment.[13] And Oliver Cowdery and Newel K. Whitney[14]—were commanded to go and visit the churches speedily—as you will see by reading the Revelation given August thirty at Kirtland[15]—The following is a copy of the Epistle written by S. Rigdons own hand.

I sidney a servant of Jesus Christ by the will of God the Father and through the faith of our Lord Jesus Christ unto the Saints who are scattered abroad in the last days, may grace [p. 34] mer[c]y and peace, rest upon you from God the father and from our Lord Jesus Christ, who is greatly to be feared, among his saints and to be had in reverance of all them who obey him.

Beloved brethren,

It has pleased God even the Father to make known unto us in these last days, the good pleasure of his will concerning his Saints; and to make known unto us, the things which he has decreed upon the nations even wasting and destruction until they are utterly destroyed, and the earth made desolate by reason of the wickedness of its inhabitants according as he has made known in times past by prophits and apostles, that such calamities should befall the inhabitants of the earth in the last days, unless they should repent and turn to the living God. And as the time is now near at hand, for the accomplishment of his purposes and the fulfilment of his prophesies, which have been spoken by all the holy prophets, ever since the world began, he has sent and signified, unto us by the mouths of his holy prophets, that. he has raised up in these last days—the speedy accomplishment of his ~~accomplish ment~~ purposes which shall be accomplished, on the heads of the rebellious of this generation—among whom he has been pleased in much mercy and goodness, to send forth the fulness of his gospel in order that they might repent and turn to the living God, and be made partakers of his Holy Spirit[.]

But by reason of their wickedness and rebellion against him and wicked and unbelieving hearts the Lord withdrew his spirit from them, and gives them up to work all uncleanness with greediness, and to bring swift destruction on themselves—[p. 35] and through their wickedness to hasten the day of their calamity, that they may be left without excuse in the day of vengeance.

But it has pleased our heavenly Father to make known some better things, concerning his Saints and those who serve him in f[e]ar and rejoice in meekness, before him, even things which pertain to life everlasting, for godliness has the ~~life~~ promise of the life, that now is, and that which is to come; Even so it has pleased our heavenly Father to make provisions for his saints in these last days of tribulation that they through faith and patience, and by continuing in well doing may preserve their lives; and attain unto rest and endless felicity—but by no other means, than that of a strict observance of his commandments and teachings in all things as there is and can be no ruler nor lawgiver in the Kingdom of God save it be God our Saviour himself—and before him he requires that all his saints & those who have named the name of Jesus, should be carful to depart from iniquity—and serve him with fe[a]r ~~and~~ rejoicing and trembling least he be angry and they perish from their way.

According to the prediction of the ancient profits that the Lord would send his messengers in the last days, and gather his elect. (which is the elect according to the covenant, viz. those who like Abraham are faithful to God and the word of his Grace.) from the four winds even from one end of the earth to the other as testified of by the Savior himself—so in these last days he has commenced to gather together, into a place provided before of God and had in reserve in days of old, being kept by the power and providence of of God, for this purpose and which he now holds in his own hands, that they through faith, and patience may inherit the ~~blessings~~ promises—A land which God by his own [p. 36] commandment has consecrated to him self where he has said, that his laws shall be kept, and where his saints can dwell in safety, through their perseverance in well doing and their unfeigned repentance of all their sins, our heavenly Father has provided this land himself because it was the one which was [best] adapted, for his children, where Jew and Gentile might dwell together: for God has the same respect to all those who call upon him in truth and righteousness whether they be Jew or Gentile; for there is no respect of persons with him.

This land being situated in the center of the continent on which we dwell with an exceeding fertile soil and ready cleared for the hand of the cultivator bespeaks the goodness of our God, in providing so goodly a heritage, and its climate suited [to] persons from every quarter of this continent. wither East West North or South yea I think I may say, for all constitutions from every part of the world and its productions nearly all varieties of both grain and vegitables which are common in this country together with all means, [for] clothing: in addition to this it abounds with fountains of pure water[,] the soil climate and surface all adapted to health[.] indeed I may say that the whole properties of the country invite the Saints to come and partake their blessings[.] but what more need I say about a country. which our Heavenly Father holds in his own hands[,] for if it were unhealthy he could make it healthy and if barren he could make it fruitful. Such is the land which God has provided for us, in these last days for an inheritance, and truly it is a goodly land, and none other as well suited for all the saints as this and all those who have faith and confidence in God who has ever seen this land will bear the same testimony. In order that you may understand the will of God respecting this land and the way and means [p. 37] of possessing it, I can only refer you to commandments which the Lord has delivered by the mouth of his Prophet which will be read, to you, by our brethren Oliver Cowdry and Newel K. Whitney whom the Lord has appointed, to visit the churches and obtain means for purchasing this land of our inheritance that we may escape in the day of tribulation which is coming on the earth. I conclude by exhorting you to hear the voice of the Lord your God, who is speaking to you in much mercy and who is sending forth, his word and his revelation in these last days, in order that we may escape impending vengeance; and the Judgements which await this generation, and which will speedily overtake them— Brethren pray for me, that I may be counted worthy to obtain an inheritance in the land of Zion and to over come, the World through faith, and dwell with the sanctified, forever, and ever Amen.

Written at Kirtland Ohio Aug. 31, 1831.

NOTES

1. D&C 52. The conference was held in Kaw Township, Jackson County, Missouri, on August 4, 1831 (*Far West Record,* 9-10; and *HC,* 1:188-89).

2. D&C 60; compare Wood, 2[1835]:198-99, where the text was included as Section 70. For background, see Cook, *Revelations,* 94-96, 143; and *HC,* 1:201-206.

3. The source for this quotation is not known.

4. Newel Knight, a son of Joseph Knight and Polly Peck, was

born on September 13, 1800, in Marlborough, Windham County, Vermont. He moved with his family to Bainbridge, New York, about 1809 and on to Colesville, New York, in 1811. He married Sally Coburn on June 7, 1825; they became the parents of three children.

Knight was baptized in May 1830 by David Whitmer and ordained a priest on September 26. In May 1831 Knight took his family and moved to Thompson, Ohio. He was ordained an elder shortly afterwards. Knight was responsible for leading the Colesville, New York, Branch to Jackson County, Missouri, to settle. The move took two months, lasting from June through July 1831. Sometime before July 3, Knight was ordained a high priest. After being ejected from Jackson County late in 1833, the Knights relocated in Clay County. Knight was appointed a member of the Clay County high council on July 7, 1834.

Sally, Newel's wife of nine years, died on September 15, 1834. Following her death, Knight returned to Kirtland, Ohio, arriving in the spring of 1835. On November 24 he married Lydia Goldthwaite, and they became the parents of seven children. While in Kirtland Knight participated in the dedication of the temple in March 1836. On April 7 the Knights left again for Missouri, arriving on May 6 in Clay County. Knight was subsequently called as a member of the high council in Far West.

Following the forced exodus of the church from Missouri in 1839, the Knights settled in Nauvoo, Illinois. Here Knight was called to be a member of the stake high council, serving in this capacity until 1845. He received his endowment in the Nauvoo temple on December 13, 1845.

Knight and his family left Nauvoo with the rest of the church under Brigham Young's direction in 1846. He died on January 11, 1847, in Knox County, Nebraska (Cook, *Revelations*, 78-79, 139; *LDSBE*, 2:773-75).

5. William W. Phelps was born on February 17, 1792, in Hanover, Morris County, New Jersey, the son of Enon Phelps and Mehitabel Goldsmith. In 1800 the family moved to Homer,

New York. Phelps married Sally Waterman on April 28, 1815; they became the parents of ten children. During this period, Phelps worked as the editor of the *Western Courier*. He and his family moved to Trumansburg, New York, in 1823, where he both edited and published a newspaper called *Lake Light*. By 1828 the family found themselves in Canandaigua, New York, and Phelps began publishing the anti-Masonic newspaper, the *Ontario Phoenix*.

Phelps's introduction to the LDS church came through the purchase of a copy of the Book of Mormon from Parley P. Pratt in 1830. He met Joseph Smith on December 21, 1830, and was baptized in 1831. Phelps and his family moved to Kirtland, Ohio, in June. From 1831 through 1838 Phelps served prominently in the church. In June 1831 he was called to serve with Oliver Cowdery in printing church literature and traveled to Jackson County, Missouri, that same summer. In August he was directed to settle in Missouri with his family. While in Jackson County Phelps served as editor for the *Evening and Morning Star*. He was also printer for the 1833 Book of Commandments. Following the expulsion of the Saints from the county in late 1833, Phelps moved his family into Clay County. On July 8, 1834, Phelps was appointed a counselor to David Whitmer in the presidency of the church over "Zion" (Missouri).

On April 25, 1835, Phelps left Clay County for Kirtland, arriving on May 16. While there he assisted in compiling the 1835 edition of the Doctrine and Covenants and in compiling and printing the first church hymnbook in 1836. He also participated in the dedication ceremonies of the Kirtland temple, writing the keynote hymn, "The Spirit of God Like a Fire Is Burning," which is found in current LDS hymnals. He left for Missouri again on April 9.

During 1836-37, with John Whitmer, Phelps began supervising the affairs of the church in Missouri independently of the high council. Their actions created confusion, and they were both excommunicated on March 10, 1838. Following his excommunication, Phelps moved to Dayton, Ohio. Here he contacted Orson Hyde and John E. Page in June 1840 and was accepted back into the church the next month. He and his family moved to Kirtland again early in 1841 where he worked to strengthen members who had been unable to emigrate with the main body of the Saints three years earlier. Following a brief preaching mission to Ohio and the eastern states in May 1841, Phelps moved his family to Nauvoo, Illinois. He was elected mayor's clerk and fire warden on February 11, 1843. He assisted the prophet as clerk, scribe, and confidant from 1841 through 1844.

On December 9, 1843, Phelps received his endowment in the Nauvoo temple; on February 2, 1846, he was sealed to Laura Stowell and Elizabeth Dunn. Phelps and his family left Nauvoo for the West with the main body of the church in 1846. On March 31, 1847, he was called to travel east and purchase a press and type. The transaction was completed in Boston the following August. Phelps returned to Winter Quarters on November 12, 1847. He was excommunicated again on December 9 but rebaptized two days later.

The Phelps family arrived in Salt Lake City in 1849. William constructed an adobe house in the Old Fort where the family resided until his death. Phelps served in the Utah territorial legislative assembly from 1841 through 1857 and was elected Speaker of the House in 1851. That same year he also became a member of the Board of Regents of the University of Deseret and published the *Deseret Almanac*. On October 7, 1851, he was admitted to the Utah bar. He wrote the lyrics to a number of other popular LDS hymns such as "Praise to the Man." He died on March 6, 1872, in Salt Lake City (Cook, *Revelations*, 87-88, 141; *LDSBE* 3:692-97).

    6. Frederick G. Williams, son of William and Ruth Granger Williams, was born October 28, 1787, at Suffield, Hartford County, Connecticut, and moved with his family to Cleveland, Ohio, about 1799. In his late youth he found employment as a pilot on Lake Erie transporting goods and passengers between

Buffalo and Detroit. Late in 1815 he married Rebecca Swain; they became the parents of four children. In 1816 the young family moved to Warrensville, Ohio, where Williams engaged in farming. By 1830 he had completed studies to become a doctor and had moved into the Kirtland area to set up his practice.

Williams was baptized into the LDS church and ordained an elder that November and accompanied the Missouri-bound missionaries to Jackson County shortly afterwards. Eight months later, in August 1831, he met Joseph Smith for the first time. Williams returned to Kirtland around September and was ordained a high priest on October 25. The following July he began serving as a scribe for Smith. He was ordained a counselor in the First Presidency on March 18, 1833.

Williams engaged in other church-related activities such as the United and Literary firms and Zion's Camp. In May 1835 he was appointed editor of a church-oriented newspaper, the *Northern Times*. He also worked on the Kirtland temple and participated in its dedication in 1836. In 1837 he became a stockholder in the Kirtland Safety Society Anti-Banking Corporation. When the bank failed, misconduct charges were brought against a number of people, including Williams. No decision was made in his case, though it strained his relationship with Smith, the bank's founder.

Williams and his family moved to Far West, Missouri, in 1837. That November he was dropped from the First Presidency and subsequently excommunicated. He was rebaptized about July 1838 and expelled from Missouri with the rest of the Saints in 1839. He was excommunicated again on March 17, 1839. The family followed the church to Quincy, Illinois, later that year, and Williams was again reinstated in the church on April 8, 1840. He died in Quincy on October 10, 1842. He was sealed to his wife Rebecca posthumously in the Nauvoo temple on February 7, 1846 (Cook, *Revelations*, 104-105, 144; *LDSBE*, 1:51-52).

7. Joseph Coe was born in 1785 in New Jersey. Sometime

before June 1831 he was baptized into the LDS church and ordained an elder. Later that month he traveled to Missouri with Joseph Smith and others. Coe returned on September 4; on September 22 he moved his family to Mentor, Ohio. From October 12-December 28 he served a mission to New York with Ezra Thayer.

On October 1, 1832, Coe was ordained a high priest by Joseph Smith; on March 18, 1833, he was ordained and set apart as an agent to purchase property for the church. On February 17, 1834, he was called to serve as a member of the Kirtland high council. Coe participated in the construction and dedication of the Kirtland temple. He assisted in laying the foundation stones on July 23, 1833, and on March 8, 1835, received a blessing for his efforts.

Coe was rejected from the Kirtland high council on September 3, 1837, and was completely disaffected by December. He was excommunicated in December 1838. The census records list him as a farmer residing in Kirtland in 1850, but further details of his life, including his death date, are not known (Cook, *Revelations*, 86-87, 141).

8. See also *HC*, 1:196-202; *Far West Record*, 9-10.

9. The elders had been in the Eastern states on a proselyting mission.

10. Emer Harris was born on May 29, 1781, in Cambridge, Washington County, New York. On July 22, 1802, he married Roxana Peas; they had six children. He married Deborah Lott on January 16, 1819; they had four children. He married Parna Chapel on March 29, 1826; they also had four children. It is not known why Harris married so many times within such a short period. It could be, as was typical of the time, that his wives died during or shortly after childbirth.

By 1820 the family had moved to Luzerne County, Pennsylvania; they were baptized into the Mormon church here on February 10, 1831. Later that year the Harrises moved to

Kirtland, Ohio. Sometime before June Harris was ordained an elder. On October 25, 1831, he was ordained a high priest. He left on a short mission with Simeon Carter on January 25, 1832; later that year he fulfilled a mission to Susquehanna County, Pennsylvania, with Martin Harris.

About December 1833 Harris moved his family to Huron County, Ohio. In 1835 he was occupied largely in constructing the Kirtland temple. In the spring of 1836 he moved his family to a farm located three miles from Kirtland. The family moved to Missouri on September 5, 1838, and arrived at Far West, Missouri, about October 12. Following the expulsion of the Mormons from Missouri the following winter, the family moved to Adams County, Illinois, about December 22. Harris purchased property about three miles northeast of Nauvoo in 1840; he was a carpenter by trade. He also served in the Nauvoo Legion.

Emer took additional wives in accordance with the law of plural marriage while living in Nauvoo. On January 11, 1846, he married Polly Chamberlain; he received his endowment in the Nauvoo temple on January 30, 1846.

In 1850 the family moved to Utah and ultimately settled in Provo. On September 10, 1850, Emer married a third wife, Martha Allen. Harris was ordained a patriarch on October 8, 1853; on September 5, 1855, he was called to preside over the high priests in Provo.

Harris died on November 28, 1869, in Logan, Cache County, Utah (Cook, *Revelations*, 154-55, 310).

11. Joseph Brackenberry was born on January 18, 1788, in Lincolnshire, England, and migrated to the United States with his family while still a child. He was baptized on April 10, 1831, by John Corrill and Solomon Hancock, and ordained an elder the next day; on October 25, 1831, he was ordained a high priest by Oliver Cowdery. Late that year he left on a mission to the Eastern States. He died on January 7, 1832, while still in the mission field, at Pomfret, Chautauqua County, New York. His death was attributed to poison administered to him by local

anti-Mormons (*LDSBE*, 2:597).

12. Wheeler Baldwin was born in March 1793, in Albany County, New York. By 1830 he had moved to Strongsville, Cuyahoga County, Ohio. He married a woman named Mary apparently while residing in Ohio. He was baptized into the Mormon church on January 8, 1831, and ordained an elder sometime before June. Baldwin was ordained to the High Priesthood on June 3, 1831, by Lyman Wight. He was appointed to travel to Missouri later that month but apparently did not go. He finally moved to Jackson County, Missouri, sometime before October 5, 1832; by 1836 Wheeler had settled his family in Caldwell County. Following the expulsion of the Mormons from the state in 1838-39, the Baldwins settled in Lee County, Iowa.

On March 6, 1840, the Iowa high council appointed Baldwin, Lyman Wight, and Abraham O. Smoot to travel and obtain affidavits and other documents to be forwarded to Washington, D.C., as part of the church's attempt to have its petitions for redress against Missouri heard in Congress.

Baldwin received his endowment in the Nauvoo temple on January 7, 1846; however, he and his family did not move West with the rest of the Saints. Several years later, around 1852, Baldwin joined Alpheus Cutler's splinter group, The Church of Jesus Christ, in Mills County, Iowa. The Baldwins moved with the Cutlerites to Manti, Fremont County, Iowa, in 1854. In March 1863 Wheeler joined the Reorganized Church of Jesus Christ of Latter Day Saints and presided over the branches of that church in the Iowa counties of Mills, Fremont, Taylor, and Page.

Wheeler Baldwin died on May 11, 1887, near Stewartsville, Missouri (Cook, *Revelations*, 72, 138; for information on the Cutlerite movement, see Steven L. Shields, *Divergent Paths of the Restoration*, 4th rev. ed. [Los Angeles, CA: Restoration Research, 1990], 60-65).

13. See D&C 58:50-51. For background, see *HC*, 1:197-98; Cook, *Revelations*, 92-93, 142.

14. Newel Kimball Whitney, son of Samuel Whitney and Susanna Kimball, was born on February 5, 1795, in Marlborough, Windham County, Vermont. In 1817 he moved to Painesville, Ohio, where he found employment with A. Sidney Gilbert, a local merchant. He later became Gilbert's business partner when the store moved to Kirtland.

On October 20, 1822, Whitney married Elizabeth Ann Smith. They had eleven children. Sometime before 1830 he joined the Campbellite movement; Sidney Rigdon was the congregation's minister. Whitney was baptized into the Mormon church in November 1830.

Whitney fulfilled a number of assignments for the church. He was ordained a bishop's agent for the Kirtland area on September 1, 1831. He was called to be the bishop of the Kirtland branch and of all the branches east of the Mississippi River on December 3, 1831. He joined the United Firm, a part of the United Order in Kirtland, on March 12, 1832. He also served on several proselyting missions. In addition, he attended the School of the Prophets in Kirtland beginning in 1833 and also helped build the Kirtland temple.

In 1838 Whitney moved his family to the Mormon settlements in Missouri. The Whitneys got as far as St. Louis when they heard about the extermination order issued by Missouri governor Lilburn W. Boggs and relocated temporarily in Carrollton, Illinois; in 1839 the family moved to Nauvoo.

Whitney served in both church and civil offices while in Illinois. He was called as bishop of the Nauvoo Middle Ward on October 6, 1839. He was elected as a city alderman on February 1, 1841. He received his endowment on May 4, 1842, participating in the first group to receive their temple ordinances. He became a member of the Council of Fifty on March 11, 1844.

Newel also participated in plural marriage. He married Emmeline Belos Woodward on February 24, 1845; they became the parents of two children. He married Elizabeth Ann, Olive Maria Bishop, Anna Houston, Elizabeth Mahala Moore, Elizabeth Almira Pond, and Abigail Augusta Pond on January 7, 1846. On

January 26 that year he married Henrietta Keys.

The Whitney family left Nauvoo for the Salt Lake Valley in 1846. After residing in Winter Quarters for some time, they finally arrived in Utah on October 8, 1848. Newel was elected a justice of the peace on March 12, 1849, and shortly afterwards was called as bishop of the Salt Lake City 18th Ward. He died September 23, 1850, in Salt Lake City (Cook, *Revelations*, 102-103; *LDSBE*, 1:222-27).

15. D&C 63:42-46; compare Wood, 2[1835]:141-45, where it appears as 20:12. For background, see Cook, *Revelations*, 98-103, 143-44.

Chapter 10

Eviction

―――

CHAPTER 10

(Immediately after the commandment was given and the epistle written O. Cowdry and N. K. Whitney went from place to place; and from Church to Church preaching and expounding the Scriptures and Commandments and obtaining ~~commandments~~ moneys of the disciples for the purpose of buying lands for the Saints [in Missouri] according to commandments and the disciples truly opened their hearts, and thus there has been lands purchased, for the inheritance of the Saints.)

Soon after this[,] the time of holding the general conference drew near and Joseph the Seer and Sidney the Scribe moved from Kirtland Ohio to Hiram Portage Co. and continued the Translation of the new [p. 38] Testament.[1] On the 25 day of Oct. 1831, the Elders assembled together at Serenes Burnets in the township of Orange and County of Cuyahaga Ohio 12 high priests — 17 elders — 5 priests and 3 teachers: at Which conference were ordained 1 elder & 14 priests the names of whom you will find <recorded> ~~an~~ [in] the the conference minute book.[2]

OCT. 1831

101

About this time it was in contemplation for Oliver Cowdry to go to Zion [Missouri] and carry with him the Revelations and Commandments, and I also received a revelation to go with him.[3] we left Ohio, on the 20 of Nov, 1831 and arrived in Zion Mo. Jan. 5, 1832.

When we arrived in Zion we found the saints in as good situation as we could reasonably expect.

Jan. 23, 1832, held a conference in Zion attended to the business of the church and licensed ten elders to go and preach the gospel.

In March 1832, the enemies held a counsel in Independence Jackson County Mo. how they might destroy the saints but did not succeed at this time, But continued their brails until they had expelld us from the county as you will hereafter see.

[—— —— —— by those from —— that we —— —— —— ——] . there are at this time 402 disciples living in this land Zion.

And it came to pass that Joseph the seer and Sidney the Scribe and N. W. Whitney and one Jesse Gause[4] came to Zion to comfort the Saints and setle some little dificulties, and regulate the church and affairs concerning it, we had a pleasant visit with them and they returned again in peace. I will here mention one circumstance and the return of these brethren while they were riding in a Stage coach the horses ran away and upset the coach and broke N. K. Whitney['s] [p. 39] ankle bone. but notwithstanding through the providence of God he soon got home, but is now somewhat infirm in consequence of aforesaid accident.[5]

About these days the Lord gave a Commandment for Joseph the seer and N. K. Whitney the Bishop at Kirtland to go and cry repentance to the cities of Boston New York and Albany. and bear testimony of their utter abolishment if they did not repent and receive the gospel.

Zion is prospering at present and high priests are stationed to watch over the several branches. December 1, 1832, there are now 538 individuals in this land belonging to the church.

And it came to pass that in the fall of the year 1832, the disciples at Ohio received the gift of tongues and in June 1833 we received the gift of tongues in Zion.⁶

About these days we received the following epistle We the undersigned citizens of Jackson County believing: that an important crisis is at hand, as regards our civil society in consequence, of a pretended religious sect of people ~~styling themselves~~ that have setled and are still setling in our County styling themselves Mormons, and intending to rid ourselves ~~as we do~~ peacefly if we can and forcibly if we must, and believing as we do, that the arm of civil law does not afford us a guarantee or at least a sufficient one, against the evils which are now inflicted upon us, and seem to be increasing by the said religious sect deem it expedient, and of the highest importance to form ourselves into a company, for the better and easier accomplishment of our purpose which we deem almost superfluous to say is Justified as well by the law of nature, as by the law of self [p. 40] preservation.

It is more than two years since the first of these fannoticks or knaves, (for one or the other they undoubtedly are) made their first appearance among us. and pretending as they did, and now do, to hold personal communion and converse face to face with the *most high* God to receive communications and revelations, direct from heaven, to heal the sick by the laying on of hands and in short, to perform all the wonder working miracles wrought by the inspired apostles and Prophets. We believe them deluded fanaticks or weak and designing knaves, and that they and their pretentions would soon pass away, but

Epistle from the citizens of Jackson County, MO.

July, 1833

in this we were deceived. The arts of a few designing leaders among them have thus far succeeded in holding them together as a society, and since the arrival of the first of them they have daily increased, and if they had been respectable citizens in society, and thus deluded, they would have been entitled to our pity rather than to our contempt and hatred, but from their appearance, from their manners, and from their conduct, since their comming among us, we have every reason to believe that with but a few very exceptions, they were of the very diggs of that society from which they came, lazy Idle and vicious[.]

This we conceive is not idle assertion but a fact susceptible of proof, For with these few exceptions above named, they brought into our country little or no property with them, and left less behind them, and we infer that those only yoked themselves to the Mormon car, who had nothing earthly or heavenly to loose by the change. and we fear that if some of the leaders among them had paid the forfeit due the crime, instead of being chosen [p. 41] embassadors of the *most high*, they would have been inmates of solitary cells. But their conduct here stamps their characters in their true color. More than a year it has been ascertained that they had been tampering with our slaves, and endeavering to sow dissension and raise sedition among them. Of this their Mormon leaders were informed, and they said they would deal with any of their members, who should again in like case offend, but how spacious are appearances in a late No. of the Star printed in Independence, by the leaders of the sect[.] there is an article inviting free negroes and mulatoes from other States to become mormons, and move and settle among us. This exhibits them in still more odious colours. It manifests a desire on the part of their society, to inflict on our society, an injury that they know would be to us entirely insuportable, and one of the surest means, of driving us from the country. for it would require none of the supernatural gifts that they pretend to, to see, that the introduction of such a cast among us, would corrupt our blacks, and instigate them to blood shed.

They openly blaspheme the *most high God*, and cast contempt on his holy religion, by pretending to receive revelations direct from heaven by pretending to speak in unknown tongues, by direct inspiration, and by divine pretentions derogotory of God and religion, and to the utter subversion of human reason.

They declare openly that God has given them this Country of land and that sooner or later they must and will have <possession of> our lands, for an inheritance and in fine they have conducted themselves, on [p. 42] many other occasions in such a manner, that we believe it a duty, we owe ourselves, to our wives and children, to the cause of public morals, to remove them from among us, as we are not prepared to give up our possesions to them, or to receive into the bosom of our families as fit companions for our wives and daughters the degraded and corrupted free negroes and mulatoes, that are now invited to setle among us.

Under such a state of things[,] even [in] our beautiful country, would [it not] cease to be a desirable residence, and our situations intolerable? We therefore agree that after timely warning, and upon receiving an adiquate compensation for what little property they cannot take with them, they refuse to leave us in peace as they found us; we agree to use such means as will be sufficient, to remove them and to that end we pledge each to each other our bodily powers, our lives, fortunes, and sacred honor.

July 15, 1833.

We will meet at the court house in the Town of Independence on Saturday next, the 20 ult: to consult of ulterior movements.

A committee was appointed at the foregoing meeting and waited on us. Partridge Corrill, Phelps <&c>. ~~Cowdry~~ &c. [met with] the committee consisted of Lewis Franklin, Mr. Campbell, Jud[ge] Lucas, Judge Fristoe, Russel Hicks, Mr. Simpson, two of the Mr. Wilsons[,] Captain Tipitts[,] & Mr. Commings.

To answer them this question will you leave this County or not? allowing us only fifteen minutes to answer the question. We did not ~~any~~ reply at that time:

The committee further required of us to shut up our printing office, store, Mechanical [p. 43] shops &c. immediately and leave the County.

Those who waited on the committee were A. S. Gilbert, Edward Partridge, Isaac Morley, John Corrill[,] W W Phelps[,] and John Whitmer

When they found that we were unwilling to comply with their requests, they returned to the Courthouse and voted to raze the printing [office] to the ground which they immediattly did. and at the same time took Edward Partridge and Charles Allen and tarred and feathered them threatning to kill us if we did not leave the County immediately.

They were also determined to demolish the store A. S. Gilbert prevailed on them to let it stand until Tuesday next and have time to pack his goods himself.

Tuesday arrived and death and destruction stared us in the face. The whole County turned out and surrounded us [and] came to W W Phelps, and my hous and took us upon the publick Square, as also Partridge, Corrill, Morly, and Gilbert and were determined to massacre us unless we agreed to leave the County immediately. Finally we agreed to leave upon the following condition.

July 23, 1833.

It is understood that the undersigned members of the said society do give their solemn pledge each for himself as follows. That Oliver Cowdery, W. W. Phelps, Wm. E. McLellin, Edward Partridge, Lyman Wight, Simeon Carter, Peter & John Whitmer, and harvey Whitlock, shall remove with their families out of this County on or before the first day ~~of Jan.~~ next and that they as well as the two herein after named use all their influence, to induce all the brethren, now here to move as soon as posible one half say by the first of Jan. next and all [p. 44] by the first day of April next and to advise and try all means in their power, to stop any more of their sect from moving to this County, as to those now on the road, and who have no notice of this agreement, they will use their influence to prevent their setling permanantly in the County but that they shall only make arrangement for temporal shelter till a new location is fixed on by the society. John Corrill & A. S. Gilbert, are allowed to remain as general agents to wind up the business of the society, so long as nesessity shall require, and said Gilbert may sell out his good[s] now on hand, but is to make no new importation. The Star is not again to be published no[r] a press set up by the society in this County.

If the said E. Partridge and W. W. Phelps move their families by the first of Jan. as aforesaid that they themselves will be allowed to go and come in order to transact and wind up their business. The committee pledge themselves, to use all their influence to prevent any violenc being used[,] so long as a compliance with the foregoing terms is observed by the parties concerned.

Signed
Samuel C. Owens   N. K. Olmstead
Leonadas Oldham   Wm. Bowers

G. W. Simpson
W. L. Irvin
John Harris
Henry Childs
Harvey H. Younger
Hugh L. Brazi<a>le

Z. Waller
Harman Gregg
Aaron Overton
Samuel Weston

The battle was fought on the evening of the [3] 4 November and only <one> of the brethren was killed & two of the mob.[7] David Whitmer headed the disciples.

[p. 45] Independence Oct. 30, 1833.

About these days we employed counsellors to assist in prosecuting the law, which we had been advised by J. Smith Jr the seer to do[.] Therefore [we] employed Donaphan, Atchison, Rees and Wood[8] of Liberty[,] Clay County[,] Mo. who engaged to carry on our Suits for $1000,00 which was agreed to be paid by E. Partridge and W W. Phelps which came from the church.

The Church was driven by the Mob of Jackson County on the 4. of November 1833. on the night of the 13th of the same month th[e] stars fell[.][9]

NOTES

1. Joseph Smith had been working on his "inspired version" of the Holy Bible. See Robert J. Matthews, *"A Plainer Translation": Joseph Smith's Translation of the Bible—A History and Commentary* (Provo, UT: Brigham Young University Press, 1975).

2. This meeting was the first of a series of special and general conferences held in Hiram, Ohio, from October 25 through November 13, 1831 (see *Far West Record*, 19-33).

3. D&C 69. In a special conference held November 12-13,

1831, the membership of the church ratified the instructions of this revelation (see *Far West Record*, 31-33).

4. Jesse Gause was born about 1785 in Pennsylvania; sometime before 1825 he married Martha Cuntry; they had five children. Gause was an active Quaker in Fayette and Chester counties in Pennsylvania and in Ohio. His wife, Martha, died in 1828. Gause married a woman named Minerva sometime before 1832; they had one child.

On April 26, 1830, Gause resigned as a Quaker preacher and sometime later that year became a member of the Shaker community in Hancock, Essex County, Massachusetts. In October 1831 the Gause family moved to Cleveland, Ohio, and joined with the Shaker community there.

Gause was baptized into the Mormon church around October 22, 1831, and was ordained a high priest on March 8, 1832; that same day he was ordained a counselor to Joseph Smith in the newly organized First Presidency of the church.

In April 1832 Jesse traveled to Independence, Missouri, with Smith and several others. He remained in Missouri after the prophet returned to Ohio in May. By August 1832 he was back in Kirtland as well.

Gause was called to serve a mission in Pennsylvania with Aebedee Coltrin in the summer of 1832; the pair left Kirtland on August 1. Gause parted company with Coltrin around August 19, apparently en route to Fayette County, Pennsylvania, where he had preached while still a Quaker. By December Gause had left the church. He was formally excommunicated on December 3, 1832 (Cook, *Revelations*, 171-72, 314-15; Robert J. Woodford, "Jesse Gause—Counselor to the Prophet," *Brigham Young University Studies* 15 [Spring 1975]: 362-64; and D. Michael Quinn, "Jesse Gause: Joseph Smith's Little-Known Counselor," *Brigham Young University Studies* 23 [Fall 1983]: 487-93).

5. Joseph Smith recorded the incident as follows:

> On the 6th of May, I gave the parting hand to the brethren in

Independence, and, in company with Brothers Rigdon and Whitney, commenced a return to Kirtland, by stage to St. Louis, from thence to Vincennes, Indiana; and from thence to New Albany, near the falls of the Ohio River. Before we arrived at the latter place, the horses became frightened, and while going at full speed, Bishop Whitney attempted to jump out of the coach, but having his coat fast, caught his foot in the wheel, and had his leg and foot broken in several places; at the same time I jumped out unhurt. We put up at Mr. Porter's public house, in Greenville, for four weeks, while Elder Rigdon went directly forward to Kirtland. During all this time, Brother Whitney lost not a meal of victuals or a night's sleep, and Dr. Porter, our landlord's brother, who attended him, said it was a pity we had not got some "Mormon" there, as they could set broken bones or do anything else. I tarried with Brother Whitney and administered to him till he was able to be moved (*HC*, I:271).

6. This refers to instances of glossolalia, or speaking in unknown tongues.

7. In Mormon history this battle has become known as the Battle of Crooked River. David W. Patten, at the time president of the Quorum of Twelve Apostles; Gideon Carter; and a young man named O'Banyon were killed. According to Pratt, Patten led the Mormon forces. See Pratt, *Autobiography*, 152-55. See also B. H. Roberts, *A Comprehensive History of the Church of Jesus Christ of Latter-day Saints, Century I*, 6 vols. (Provo, UT: Brigham Young University Press, 1965), 1:314-47; Warren A. Jennings, "Zion Is Fled: The Expulsion of the Mormons from Jackson County, Missouri," Ph.D. diss., University of Florida, 1962; and Richard L. Bushman, "Mormon Persecutions in Missouri, 1833," *Brigham Young University Studies* 3 (Autumn 1960): 11-20.

[handwritten margin note: This is grossly inaccurate off by several years as this didn't occur until Oct. 1838]

8. For more on Alexander W. Doniphan, David R. Atchison, et al., and this episode, see Stephen L. LeSueur, *The 1838 Mormon War in Missouri* (Columbia: University of Missouri Press, 1987), 77-89.

9. There was a meteor shower.

Chapter 11
"Your Humble Petitioners"

CHAPTER XI

The situation of our brethren after leaving their homes in Jackson in the most distressing circumstances, in the cold month of November found it difficult to preserve life in many instances, some fled with but few clothes, leaving their beds and bedding, others taking with them what they could carry, and running for their lives, women losing some of their children while fleeing for their lives and thus you may Judge how the poor saints have suffered after having given only a few hints of the distress.

You will find in one of the Nos of the Star printed at Kirtland[,] Ohio[,] a piece headed the mormons which will serve to illustrate (to be published.) Dated Feb. 1834.

I would here remark that a full account of the proceedings of the Jackson Mob is published in the Star at Kirtland commencing at No. 15. to the end of the volume.
[p. 46] Liberty Clay County Feb. 19, 1834

To the Judge John S. Ryland of the 5th circuit of Mo.

Sir learning that a court of inquiry is to be held in Jackson

Co. at the next regular term of the circuit Court for the Co. or that some kind of legal proceedings is to Commence, for the purpose of obtaining the facts, as far as can be, to the criminal transactions and rioutous procedings, or bringing to punishment the guilty in that County[.]

We therefore pray your honour to avail yourself of every means in your power to execute the law and make it honorable, and believing that the testimony of some of the members of our church will be important, and deeming it unsafe to risk our persons in that County without a guard, we request that the order from the Executive already transmited, may be put in force[.]

Respectfully
Edward Partridge
W. W. Phelps
John Whitmer
A. S. Gilbert
John Corrill.

Clay County April 9, 1834.
Dear Sir [Governor Dunklin]:
Not with standing you may have become tired of receiving communications from us, yet we beg leave of your excellency to pardon <us> of this as we have this week enclosed a petition to the president of the United States (A[ndrew]. Jackson) setting forth our distressed conditions together with your [p. 47] excellencys views of it as well as the limited powers, with which your are clothed, to afford that protection, which we need to enjoy our rights and lands in Jackson County. A few lines from the Governor of this state, in connection with our humble entreaties for our possessions and privileges, we think would be of considerable consequence towards bringing

about the desired object, and would be gratefully acknowledged by us, and our society, and we may add by all honorable men.

We therefore as humble petitioners ask the favor of your excellency to write to the President (A. Jackson,) of the U.S.A. that he may assist us, or our society in obtaining our rights in Jackson Co., and help protect us, when there, till we are safe.

Are in duty bound, we will pray.

                                        W W Phelps
                                        E. Partridge
                                        John Whitmer

Daniel Dunklin   John Corrill
Gov. Of Mo.   A. S. Gilbert

Liberty Clay County Mo. April 10, 1834
    To the president of the United States of America

We the undersigned, your humble petitioners Citizens of the United States of America being members of the Church of Christ reproachfully called Mormons, beg leave to refer the president to our former petition dated Oct. last. and also to lay before him the accompanying hand bill, dated December It, 1833, with assurances [p. 48] that the said handbill exhibits but a faint sketch of the suffering of your petitioners and their brethren, up to the period of its publication[.]

The said handbill shows that at the time of dispersion part of our families fled into the new and unsetled Co. of Vanburen being unable to procure provisions in that Co th[r]ough the winter[.] many of them were compelled to return to their homes in Jackson Co. or perish with hunger But they had no sooner set foot upon that soil, which a few months before we had purchased of the United States, then they were again met by the Citizens of Jackson Co. and a renewal of savage barbarity inflicted upon them, by beating with clubs and sticks, presenting knives and fire arms and threatning with death if they did not immediate flee from the Co. These inhuman assaults upon these families were repeated two or three times through the last winter, till they were compelled at last to leave their possessions, in Jackson Co. and flee with their mangled bodies, in to this Co. (Clay.) Here to mingle their tears and unite their supplications with hundreds of their brethren to our Heavenly Father, and the Chief ruler of our nation.

Between one and two thousand of the people called mormons, have been driven by the force of arms, from the Co. of Jackson, in this state since the first of Nov. last being compelled to leave their highly cultivated fields the greater part of which had been bought of the United States, and of all this [because] of our belief in direct revelation from God to the children of men, according to the Holy [p. 49] Scriptures[.] we know that such illegal violence has not been inflicted upon any sect or community of people by the citizens, of the United States since the decleration of Independence.

That this is a religeous pursecution, is notorious throughout our country, where accomplices in these unparallelled outrages, engaged in the destruction of the Printing office, Dwelling house &c. yet the records of the Judicial tribunals of that County, are not stained by a crime by our people. Our numbers being greatly inferior to the enemy, we were unable to stand in self defence. And our lives at this day are continually threatened by that infuriated people, so that our personal safety forbids <one of> our members going into that County on business.—We beg leave to state that no impartial investigation into this criminal matter can be made, because the offenders must be tried in the County in which the offence was commited, and the inhabitants of the county both magistrates and people, being combined, with the exception of a few,

Justice cannot be expected.—At this day your petitioners do not know of a Solitary family belonging to our Church but what have been violently expelled from Jackson Co. by the inhabitants thereof.—Your petitioners have not gone into detail with an account of their individual sufferings from death and bruised bodies and the universal distress which prevails at this day in a greater [p. 50] or less degree, throuout our whole body not only because those sacred rights are guaranteed to every religeous sect, have been publically invaded in open hostility to the spirit and genius of our free government, but such of their houses as have not been burned their beds and most of their products of the labor of their hands for the last year have been wrested from them by a band of out laws, congregated in Jackson Co. on the western boundaries of the State of Missouri—within about thirty miles of the United States Military Post at Fort Leavenworth on the Missouri River. Your petitioners say that they do not enter into a minute detail of their sufferings in this petition least they should weary the patience of their *Venerable Chief* whos ordious [arduous] duties they know, are great and daily accumulating.

We only hope to show to him that this is an unprecedented emergency in the history of our country—that the magistracy thereof is set at defiance and Justice checked in the open violation of its laws and that we your petitioners, who are almost wholy native born citizens of these U. S. A., of whom they purchased their lands in Jackson Co. Mo. with intent to cultivate the same, as peacible citizens, are now forced from them, and dwelling in the Counties of Clay[,] Ray and Layfayette in the State of Mo without permanant homes, and suffering all the privations which must nessessarily result from such inhuman treatment, Under [p. 51] these sufferings, your petitioners, petitioned the Governor of this State in December last, in answer to which they receved the following letter. City of Jefferson Feb 4, 1834.[1] ~~by the fore going letter from the Governor, the president will forgive a disposition manifested by him~~

Your communication of the 6th Decm. was regularly recieved, and duly considered, and had I not expected to receive the evidenc brought out on the enquired ordered into the Military conduct of Col. Pitcher in a short time after I received your petition, I should have replied long since.

Last evening I was informed that the further enquiry of the court, was postponed until the 20, inst, Then before I can have any thing from this court, the court of civil Jurisdiction, will hold its session in Jackson Co. [and] consequently cannot recieve any thing from one preparatory to arrangement from the other.

I am very sensible indeed indeed of the injury your people complain of, and should consider myself very amiss in the discharge of my dutyes even, were I not to do every thing in my power consistent with the legal exercise of them, to afford your society redress to which they seem entitled, one of your requests needs no evidence to support the right to have it granted, it is, that your people be put in possession of their homes from which they have been expelled. But what may be the duties of the Executive after that, will [p. 52] will depend upon contingencies. If upon enquiry it is found your people were wrongfully dispossessed of their arms of Col. Pitcher, then an order will be issued to have them returned; and should your men organize according to law, which they have a right to do, (indeed it is their duty,) to do so, unless exempted by religious scruples.) and apply for public arms, the Executive could not distinguish between their rights to have them and the right of any other description of people similarly situated.

As the request for keeping up a military force, to protect your people and prevent the commission of crimes, were I to comply it would transend the powers with which the Executive of this State is clothed[.]

The federal Constitution has given to Congress the power to provide for calling forth the Militia to execute the laws of the Union, suppress insurrections or impel invasions, and for these purposes the President of the United States is authorized to make the call upon the Executive of the respective States. And the laws of the state empower "the Commander in Chief in case of actual or threatened invasion[,] insurection or war, or public danger, or other emergency, to call forth into actual service, such portion of the Militia as he may deem expedient." These together with the general provisions in our State constitution that, "the Governor shall take care that the laws are faithfully executed," and call upon this bra[nch] of Executive power. None of these as I [p. 53] consider embrace this part of your request. The "Words, or other emergencies," in our Militia law, seem quite broad, but the immergency to come within the object of that provision should be of a public nature. Your case is certainly a very emergent one, and the consequences as important to *your society* as if the war had been waged against the whole State, yet the public has no other interest in it than that the laws be faithfully executed, this for, I presume the whole community feel a deep interest, for that which is the case of the *Mormons* of to day may be the case of the *Catholics* tomorow, & and after them any other sect that may become obnoctious, to a majority of the people of any Section of the State. So far as a faithful execution of the laws are concerned, the Executive is disposed to do every thing consistent with the means furnished him by the Legislature and I think, I may safely say the same of the Judiciary.

As now advised I am of opinion that a Military guard will be nescessary to protect the State witnesses and officers of the Court, and to assist in the execution of its orders while sittin in Jackson County, By this mail I write to Mr Rees embracing him an order and the Capt. of the "Liberty Blues." requiring the Capt, to comply with the requisition of the Circuit Attorney in protecting the Court and officers, and executing their precepts and orders, during the process of the trials. Under the protection of this guard, your people can if they [p. 54] think proper, return to their homes in Jackson County, and be protected in them during the progress of the trials in question, by which time facts will be developed upon which I can act more definitely. The attorney general will be required to assist the Circuit attorney, if the latter deems it neccessary.

On the subject of Civil injuries, I must refer you to the Courts, such questions rest with them exclusively. The laws are sufficient to afford a remedy for every injury of this kind, and whenever you make out a case entitling you to damages, there can be no doubt entertained of their ample award. Justice is sometimes Slow in its progress, but it is not less sure on this account.

 To Messrs.   Very Respectfully your
 W. W. Phelps   (Signed)   Obt. Servt.
 Isaac Morley   Daniel Dunklin.
 John Whitmer
 Edward Partridge
 John Corrill and
 A. S. Gilbert

By the foregoing letter from the Governor will perceive a disposition manifested by him to enforce the laws as far as means have been furnished by the Legislature of this State, But the powers vested in the Executive of this State seem to be inadequate for relieving the distresses, of your petitioners in this present emergency. He is willing to send a guard to conduct our families back to their possessions but is not authorized to direct a military force, to be stationed any length of time, [p. 55] for the protection of your petitioners. this step would be laying a more fatal tragedy than the first, as our numbers at present are to small to contend single handed with the Mob of said County.—And as the federal constitution has given to congress, the power to provide for calling forth the Militia to execute the laws of the Union, suppress insurrections, or repel invasions.—"And for these purposes, the President of the United States is authorized to make the call upon the Executive of the respective States." Therefore we your petitioners in behalf of our Society, which is so scattered, and suffering, most humbly pray that we may be restored to our lands, houses and property in Jackson County, and protected in them by an armed force till peace can be restored, and as in duty bound we will ever pray.

Signed by 51 leading members of said Church.

Liberty Clay Co. Mo   April 10. 1834.[2]
To the President of the U.S.A.

We the undersigned whose names are subscribed to the accompanying petition, some of the leading members of the church of Christ, beg leave to refer the president to the handbill and petition here with. We are not insensible of the multiplicity of business, and numerous petitions, by which care and perplexity of our Chief Ruler is daily increased; and it is with difidence that we venture to lay before the Executive at this emergent period these two documents, wherein is briefly portrayed, the most unparallelled persecution [p. 56] and flagrant outrage of law that has disgraced our country since the declaration of Independence. But knowing the independent fortitude and vigorous energy, for preserving the rights of the Citizens of this Republic, which has hitherto marked course of our Chief Magistrate, we are encouraged to hope, that this communication will not pass unnoticed, but that the President, will consider our locations on the extreme frontier of the United States, exposed to many ignorant and lawless ruffians, who are already congregated, and determined to nullify all law, that will procure to your petitioners the privilege of a peacible possession of their lands in Jackson Co.

We again repeat, that our Society is wandering in adjoining counties at this day, bereft of their houses and lands, and threatened with death by the aforesaid outlaws, of Jackson Co. And lest the President should be deceived in regard to our true situation, by the misrepresentations of certain individuals, who are disposed to cover the gross outrages of the *Mob*, from *religeous, Political,* and *speculative* motives, we beg leave to refer him to the Governor of Mo. at the same time informing him that the <number of> men composing the mob of Jackson Co. may be estimated at from three to five hundred most of them, prepared with fire arms.—

After noting the statements here made, if it should be the disposition of the President, to grant aid, we most humbly entreat, that early relief may be extended to suffering families, who are now expelled from their [p. 57] possessions by firearms.—Our lands in Jackson Co; are about thirty miles distant from Fort Leavenworth, on the Mo. River.

With due respect we are

Sir your Obt. Servt.
A. S. Gilbert

W. W. Phelps
Edward Partridge
John Whitmer
John Corrill

P.S.

In Feb. last a number of our people were marched under a guard furnished by the Governor of the State into Jackson Co. for the purpose of prosecuting the *mob* criminally but the Attorney General of the State, and the District Attorney, knowing the force and power of the Mob, advised us to relinquish all hopes, of criminal prosecution to affect anything against the band of outlaws, and we returned under Guard without the least prospect of our obtaining our rights and possessions in Jackson Co. with any other means than a few companies of the United States <regular> troops, to guard and assist us, until we are safely setled.

Signed by the same as the foregoing.

Liberty Clay Co. Mo. April 24, 1834.
Dear Sir [Governor Dunklin]:

In your last communication of the 9th ints we omited to make enquiry concerning the evidence brought up before [p. 58] the court of enquiry, in the Case of Col. Pitcher, the Court met pursuant to adjournment on 20 of Feb. last and for some reason unknown to us, we have not been able to ascertain information concerning the opinion or decision of the Court.—We had hoped that the testimony would have been transmitted to your Excellency before this, that an order might be issued for the return of our arms, of which we have been wrongfully dispossessed, as we believe will clearly appear to the commander in Chief when the evidence is laid before him.—as suggested in your communication of Feb. 4, [W]e had concluded to organize according to law, and apply for public arms, but we feared that such a step, which must be attended with public ceremonies, might produce some excitement. We have thus far delayed any movement of that nature, hoping to regain our arms from Jackson Co. that we might independently equip ourselves and be prepared to assist in the maintainance of our constitutional rights and liberties as guaranteed to us by our Country, and also to defend our persons and property from a lawles *mob*, when it shall please the executive, at some future day, to put us in possession of our homes, from which we have been most wickedly expelled, We are hapy to make an expression of thanks for the willingness manifested by the executive to enforce the laws as far as he can constitutionally, "with the means furnished him by the Legislature," and we are firmly pursuaded that a future day will [p. 59] verify to him, that whatever aid we receive from the Executive, has not been lavished upon a band of traitors, but upon a people whose respects and veneration for the laws of our country, and its pure republican principles are as great as that of any other society in these United States.

As our Jackson foes, and their correspondants are busy in circulating slanderous and wicked reports concerning our people their views &c. we have deemed it expedient to inform your Excellency that we have received communications from our [people] at the East, informing us, that a number of brethren, perhaps 2 or 3 hundred, would come to Jackson Co. in the course of the ensuing season, and we are satisfied that when the Jackson mob get the inteligence, that a large number of our people are about to remove into that County, they will raise a great hew and cry, and circulate many bug bears[3] through the medium of their favorite press. But we think your Excellency is well aware that our object is purely to defend ourselves, and possessions, against another unparalleled attack from that *mob*. in as much as the Executive of this State cannot keep a military force "to protect our people in that County without transcending his powers." We want therefore the privilege of defending ourselves, and the constitution of our country while God is willing we should have a being on his footstool. We do not now know at what [time] our friends from the east will arrive, but ex [p. 60] pect more certain inteligence in a few weeks. Whenever they do arrive, it would be the wish of our people, in this Co., to return to our homes in company with our friends, under guard, and when once <more> in legal possession of our homes in Jackson Co. we will endeavor to take care of them, without further wearying the patience of our worthy Chief Magistrate. We will write hereafter or send an express—during the intermediate time, we would be glad to hear of the prospect of recovering our arms.

With due Respect
We are, Sir:
Your Obt. servt.
A. S. Gilbert
W W. Phelps
E. Partridge
John Corrill
J. Whitmer

NOTES

1. The legal options the governor proposes here had already been exhausted by the time this petition to the president was made.

2. This cover letter accompanied the preceding petition.
3. False stories.

Chapter 12

The Court of Public Sentiment

CHAPTER 12.

May 10, 1838.

I will here remark that the Saints are and were preparing, to go back to Jackson Co. as soon as the way should open. we had ~~had~~ [a] hard [time] strugling to obtain a living as may well be understood, being driven having no money, or means to subsist upon, and being among stranger[s] in a strang place, being despised, mocked at and laughed to scorn by some, and pitied by others, thus we lived from Nov 1833 until May 1834. And had little prospect [p. 61] yet to return to our homes in Jackson Co. in safety—the mob rages, and the peoples hearts are hardened, and the Saints are few in number, and poor, afflicted, caust out, and smitten by their enemies.

I will further state because of the scattered situation and the many perplexities I am not in possession of all the letters and information that I wish I was, and some that are in my possession are not arranged according to date because of the situation I am in being poor, and write as I can obtain inteligence, and find time between sun and sun to write.

City Jefferson April 20, 1834
    To Messrs.
Phelps, Partridge,
Corrill, Whitmer and
Gilbert.   Gentlemen

Yours of the ninth inst, ~~by~~ was received yesterday, in which you request me, as Executive of this State, to Join you in an appeal, to the President of the United States, for protection in the enjoyment of your rights, in Jackson Co. [I]t will readily occur to you, no doubt, the possibility of having asked of the President, in a way that he no more than the Executive of this State could render, If you have petitioned for that which I would be of opinion, he has power to grant, I should have no objection to Join in urging it upon him. But I could [p. 62] no more ask the President, however willing I am to see your society restored to and protected in their rights, to do that which I think he has no power to do, than I would do such an act myself. If you will send me a copy of your petition to the President, I will Judge of his right to grant it; and if of the opinion he possess the power, I will write in favour of its exercise.

I am now in corispondance with the Federal Government, on the subject of deposits of munitions of War, on our Northern and Western boundaries, and have no doubt but shall succeed in procuring one, which [will] be located if left to me, (and the Secretary of war seems willing to be governed by the opinion of the Executive of this State.) Some where near the state line either in Jackson or Clay Counties,

The establishment will be an ("Arsenal") and will probably be under the command of [a] Lieutenant of the army. This will afford you the best means of military protection the nature of your case will admit. Although I can see no direct impropriety in making the subject of this paragraph public yet I should prefer it not to be so considered, for the present, as the erection of an arsenal is only in expectancy.

 Permit me to suggest to you, that as you have now greatly the advantage over your enemies, in *public estimation*, that there is a great propriety in retaining that advantage, which you can easily do, by keeping [p. 63] your advisaries in the wrong. The law both civil and Military, seem to be deficient in affording your society proper protection, nevertheless *public sentiment* is a powerful corrective of error, and you should make it your policy to continue to deserve it.

With much respect, and
great regard I am your
Obt. Servt.
Daniel Dunklin

(signed)

City of Jefferson May 2, 1834
To Messrs
 W W Phelps & others

      Gentlemen

 Yours of the 24 ult. is before me; in reply to which, [I] can inform you that becoming impatient at <delay> the court of enquiry in making their report in the case of Lieut. Col. Pitcher — on the 11 ult. I wrote to General Thompson for the reason of such delay, [and] last night I received his reply, and with it the report of the court of enquiry, from the tenor of which, I find no dificulty, in deciding that the arm[s] your people [were] required to surrender on the fifth of Nov. should be returned; and have issued an order to Col. [Samuel D.] Lucas, to deliver them to you or to your order. which order is here enclosed.

                    Respectfully your
                        Obt. Srvnt.
(signed)   Daniel Dunklin

[p. 64]   City Jefferson May 2, 1834.
To S. D. Lucas,
Col. 33. Reg.

                    Sir

The court orderd to enquire into the Conduct of Lieu. Col. Pitcher in the movement he made on the 5th Nov. last, report it as their unanimaus opinion that there was no *insurrection* on that day; and that Lieu. Col. Pitcher, was not authorized to to call out <his> troops on the 5th Nov. 1833.—It was unnessessary to require the mormons to give up their arms. Therefore you will deliver to W. W. Phelps, Edward Partridge, John Corrill, John Whitmer and A. S. Gilbert, or their order The fifty-two guns and one pistle reported, by Leiu. Col. Pitcher to you on the fifth Decem. last, as having been received by him from the Mormons on the 5th of the preceeding Oct.

                    Respectfully
                        Daniel Dunklin
                        Commander in Chief

Libert[y] Clay Co. May 7, 1834
Dear sir:

Your favor of the 20. ult came to hand the first instant, which gives us a gleam of hope that ~~our~~ the time will come when we may experience a partial mitigation of our sufferings. The salutary advice in the conclusion of your letter is received with great deference.

Sinc our last of the 24 ult. the Mob of Jackson Co. have

burned our dwellings, as near as we can ascertain between 100 and 150 were consumed by fire in about one [p. 65] week[.] our arms were also taken from the depository (the Jail) about ten days sinc, and distributed among the mob. Great efort are now [in the] making by the mob to stir up the Citizens of this County, and Layfayette to commit similar outrages against us, but we think they will fail in accomplishing their wicked designs in this Co. we here annex a copy of the petition to the president.

With great respect.
Your Obt Servt

signed

A. S. Gilbert
W W Phelps.

Liberty May 15, 1834.
Col. D. S. Lucas
                Sir:

                We have this day received a communication from the Governor of this State covering the order here with, and we hasten to for word the said order to you by the bearer Mr. Richardson, who is instructed to receive your reply.

We would further remark that under existing circumstances we hope to receive our arms on this side the River, and we would name a place near one of the ferries for your convineaince—As the arms are few in number, we request that they may be delivered as soon as possible.

Respectfully yours,
A. S. Gilbert, W. W. Phelps,
J. Corrill, E. Partridge
John Whitmer

Chapter 13
The Armies of Israel

[P. 66] CHAPTER 13

June 1, 1834.

    The Jackson County *mob*, have sent a Mr. Samuel Campbell to harangue the people of Clay County on the subject of Mobocracy. For they anticipated that they needed help, therefore, they sent runners in the adjoining Counties to strengthen themselves against the day when the Camp[1] should arrive, I mean the company headed by Joseph Smith Jr. the Seer, who were now on their way to this land. Campbell succeeded in embittering the minds of some, and the Idea that Joseph should venture to bring an armed force into this uper country to afford relief to the poor and afflicted saints, enraged the enemy, and darkness, gloom, and consternation pervaded the countenance of every enemy that was sen[t] in this uper country, some said they were fearful of the consequence of such a bold an attempt. others were fearful of their lives and fortune and thus it was.

    The aforesaid Campbell had a petition to get signors, to turn o[u]t and help them, he, went from place to place, and held meetings for that purpose, but obtained only about 20 signors in Clay Co.

The Saints here are preparing with all possible speed to arm themselves and otherwise prepare to go to Jackson Co. when the Camp arrives, for we have had some hints from Joseph the Seer that this will be our privilege: so we were in hopes that the long wished for day will soon arrive. [p. 67] and Zion be redeemed to the Joy and satisfaction of the poor suffering saints.

The mob of Jackson Co proposed to sell to us, or buy our possessions in a manner that they knew that we could not comply with, if we were ever so willing, which served to blind the mind of those who had heretofore said nothing, but now advised us to comply because they thought we had better have something than nothing for our possessions.

The camp now arrived at Fishing River, where the enemy desired to head them being led by Priests &c. But God interposed and sent a storm of Thunder lightning and rain at an astonishing rate. Which stoped our enemies in consequence of the flood of water which swelled the River and made it impassable. Joseph the Seer had frequently exhorted the saints on their way up that if they would not heed his words the Lord would scourge them. The Cholera broke out in the camp an[d] several died with it to the grief and sorrow of the brethren—and lamentation of their wives and families. The Camp immediately scattered in the Counties of Ray and Clay. some returned immediately, while others tarried.

[Joseph] Received a revelation that it was not wisdom to go to Jackson county at this time and that the armies of Israel should become very great and terrable first, and [only after] the Servants of the Lord [had] been <en>dowed with power from on high previous to the Redemption of Zion.[2]

Thus our fond hopes of being redeemed at this [p. 68] time

were blasted at least for a season.

The first Elders were to receive their endowment[3] at Kirtland Ohio in the house of the Lord built in that stake.[4]

NOTES

1. The history of the relief effort sent to the Saints in Missouri from Kirtland, known as Zion's Camp, is covered in *HC*, 2:61-123; B. H. Roberts, *A Comprehensive History of the Church of Jesus Christ of Latter-day Saints, Century I*, 6 vols. (Provo, UT: Brigham Young University Press, 1965), 1:357-68; Backman, *Heavens*, 162-200; and Peter Crawley and Richard L. Anderson, "The Political and Social Realities of Zion's Camp," *Brigham Young University Studies* 14 (Summer 1974): 406-20.

2. D&C 105. This section was not included in the Doctrine and Covenants until the 1844 Nauvoo edition (see Cook, *Revelations*, 212-14, 326).

3. Ritual washings and anointings. These were expanded in Nauvoo, Illinois, to comprise the temple endowment.

4. The equivalent of a Catholic diocese.

Chapter 14

Retreat to Kirtland

CHAPTER 14.

Joseph the seer began to set in order the Church in this country.

Commenced to organize a high counsel [in Missouri] according to the Patron [pattern] received in Kirtland[,] Ohio. After which Joseph Smith Jr. F[rederick]. G. Williams and others returned to Kirtland and the Saints remained in their places of abode to wait the due time of the Lord to be redeemed from wicked mobbers.[1]

We the inhabitants of Zion wrote an appeal signed by W. W. Phelps; David Whitmer, John Whitmer, E. Partridge, John Corrill, I. Morl[e]y, P. P. Pratt, Lyman Wight, Newel Knight, T[homas]. B. Marsh, Simeon Carter and Calvin Bebee. Missouri July 1834 and Published at Kirtland in an extra Star Aug. 1834 (insert here)

The above appeal and the following petition was accompanied. The petition reads as follows.

To his Excellency Daniel Dunklin Governor of the State of Mo.

The undersigned respect fully show.

That a large number of the citizens of the United States, inhabitants of the State of Mo. professing to be the Church of latter day saints, [p. 69] wrongfully called "Mormons," having been illegally and cruelly been driven from their lands and homes, in Jackson Co. Mo. by a lawless mob. (as your excellency has already been informed.) should by some ample means be restored, to their possessions and rights: But as the said mob of Jackson Co has considerably spread itself and organized into an independant branch of government, by appointing a "commander in chief," and by preparing to resist the said church even to blood shed, and that too, with not only the common weapons used for self defence and military discipline, But with "Cannon."—Therefore your petitioners humbly ask your Excellency, while the said church is preparing to return, to petition the President of the United States for a guard of troops to be stationed in Jackson Co. sufficient to protect this unfortunate people in thier rights as well as imposing enough to quell the Jackson Co. *Mob*, for the honor of the State of Mo.

In asking this favor of the Governor while such great *mob* as that of July last in the City of N. York, and others; in other States, have been promptly put down by Military or other exhertion, your petitioners feel confident, that he will use all honorable means, to restore this suffering body of citizens to all their constitutional rights and enjoyments, for the good of society and the safety of freemen, at the same time sparing no pains to bring mobbers to Justice, and crush mobbing [p. 70] in a country which professes to be governed by wholesome laws; and your petitioners will ever pray.

While all the foregoing letters and petitions were circulating the saints were humbling themselves before the Lord. but some were making preperation to leave the land others, were doubting the truth of the book of Mormon, others denying the faith, others growing in grace and <in> the knowledge of the truth.

April 28, 1835.
This day myself and family ~~by~~ in company with W. W. Phelps and his son Waterman started for Kirtland[,] Ohio[,] in obedience to the direction of Joseph the Seer.[2]

Pretty much all the first Elders had left for Kirtland ~~on~~ previous to our going. some went on a tour preaching in their several courses.

While we were in trouble in Mo. the saints in Kirtland[,] Ohio[,] had trouble also; but God had decreed to keep a strong hold in Kirtland for five years therefore the wicked did not prevail, and the house of the Lord was building and the Saints gathering and preparing for the great day when the Lord should condecend to endow his first elders. according to his promises. That his work might roll forth and be established according to his decree in the last [p. 71] days, that he might gather together his elect from the four quarters of the earth and be prepared when the veil of the coming of all flesh shall be taken off or away, and Zion become the Joy of all the earth.

Arrived at Kirtland the 17 of May. found the brethren in good health and spirits and prospering the house of the Lord was reared and the stonework thereof completed the rafters were just put up and the first story of the steeple raised.

NOTES

1. *HC*, 2:122-26, 135, 139; *Far West Record*, 70-74.

2. See the minutes of a meeting held June 23, 1834, where these men were selected to go to Kirtland and participate in the washings and anointings that constituted the "endowment" at that time (*Far West Record*, 68-70).

Chapter 15
Twelve Apostles

CHAPTER 15

Kirtland Ohio May 26, 1835.

Soon after our arrival in this place we held many counsels, an[d] in particular I will here notice [those] in which were several selections made, for particular individuals according to the dictation of the Spirit of the Lord through Joseph the Revelator. for inheritances in Zion[1] as follows. first,

Martin Harris 1	Hiram Smith 11
J. Smith Jr 2	J. Smith Sen. 12
Oliver Cowdery 3	Peter Whitmer sr. 13
David Whitmer 4	John Whitmer 14
Sidney Rigdon 5	F. G. Williams 15
Edward Partridge 6	W. W. Phelps 16
Isaac Morley 7	S[amuel]. H. Smith 17
John Corrill 8	Wm. Smith 18[2]
N. K. Whitney 9	D. C. Smith 19
Reynolds Cahoon 10	Christian Whitmer 20

[p. 72]
Jacob Whitmer 21
Peter Whitmer Jr 22
Joseph Knight 23
Newel Knight 24
Joseph Knight Jr. 25
Hezekiah Peck 26
Ezekiel Peck 27
Philo Dibble 28
Calvin Bebee 29
Isaaih Bebee 30
Titas Billings 31
T[homas]. B. Marsh 32
Hiram Page 33
Simeon Carter 34
Jared Carter 35
Soloman Daniels 36
J. M. Burk 37
P. P. Pratt 38
Orson Pratt 39
John Murdock 40
John Johnson 41
Luke Johnson 42
Lyman E. Johnson 43
Orson Hyde 44
Joshua Lewis 45
Soloman Hancock 46
Levi Hancock 47
Zebedee Coltrin 48
Lyman Wight 49
Joseph Coe 50
Daniel Stanton 51
Freeborn Demillo 52
Lewis Abbot 53
Jesse Hitchcock 54
John Smith 55
Adolphus Chapin 56
Able Pryer 57
George Pitkin 58
Truman Brace 59
Edmund Durfee 60
Brigham Young 61
A. C. Grant 62
David Pettegrew 63

Some time in may the twelve apostle[s] were Chosen,[3] and

ordained according to revelation given to D[avid]. Whitmer and Oliver [p. 73] Cowdery[4]

The following are the names of the twelve[5]
T[homas]. B. Marsh
D[avid]. W. Patten[6]
P[arley]. P. Pratt
Orson Hyde[7]
H[eber]. C. Kimball[8]
Orson Pratt
Luke Johnson[9]
L[yman]. E. Johnson[10]
Brigham Youngs[11]
W[illiam]. E. Mc Lellin
J[ohn]. F. Boyinton.[12]

On the morning of the fifth of May the twelve took leave of their families and brethren, to fill their first mission under this commission, being commissioned to carry the gospel to Gentile and also unto Jew. having the keys of the gospel to unlock and then call on others to promulgate the same.

About the same time there were 70 high priests chosen, who were called Elders, to be under the direction of the twelve and assist them according to their needs, and if seventy were not enough, [they were to] call 70 more until 70 times 70.

Out of the first 70 were selected chosen and ordained for Presidents 7, viz.
Zebidee Coltrin 1[13]
Sylvester Smith 2[14]
Leonard Rich 3[15]
[p. 74] Hazen Aldrich 4[16]
Joseph Young 5[17]
Lyman Sherman 6
Levi Hancock 7[18]

The charge given by Oliver Cowdery, David Whitmer, and Martin Harris, together with their blessings you will find recorded in the history kept by the twelve and also by the Seventies.[19]

NOTES

1. "Inheritances in Zion" refers to the rewards—usually property—the faithful were to receive. The number to the side of each name refers to their order within the list.

2. William Smith, younger brother of the prophet Joseph Smith, was born on March 13, 1811, in Royalton, Windsor County, Vermont. He was baptized into the church June 9, 1830, by David Whitmer and ordained a teacher on October 5. On October 25, 1831, following the family's move to Ohio earlier that year, William was ordained a priest; on December 19, 1832, he was ordained an elder by Lyman E. Johnson. On June 21, 1833, William was ordained a high priest.

Smith married Caroline Amanda Grant on February 14, 1833; they had two children.

In 1834 William marched to Missouri with Zion's Camp. On February 15, 1835, following the disbanding of the Camp and his subsequent return to Ohio, Smith was ordained an apostle and made a member of the original Quorum of the Twelve. In connection with his new calling, Smith filled a mission to the eastern states with the rest of the Twelve during the summer and fall of 1835.

Like others during this period, William's faith in the new religion wavered. On October 30, 1835, he was charged with possessing a "rebellious spirit." In a revelation dated November 3, 1835, he was called upon to humble himself and repent. Smith was tried for "unchristian conduct" on January 2, 1836, but the next day he confessed his sins and was forgiven.

During the winter of 1835-36 William attended the Hebrew

School in Kirtland. In March 1836 he participated in the dedication of the Kirtland temple. He became a charter member of the Kirtland Safety Society Anti-Banking Corporation in January 1837.

On September 27, 1837, William left Kirtland with the prophet Joseph and several others for a trip to Caldwell County, Missouri; they arrived late in October. William returned home to Kirtland shortly afterwards to prepare his family for the move to Missouri. They left in the spring of 1838. Following the expulsion of the Mormons from the state of Missouri during the winter of 1838-39, the family settled in Plymouth, Illinois.

While living in Illinois, Smith's faith continued to wax and wane. He was disfellowshipped on May 4, 1839, then restored to full fellowship on May 25. When the Quorum of the Twelve left to serve a mission in the British Isles that summer, William refused to go. He did, however, serve another mission in the eastern states in the summer of 1843, returning to Nauvoo on April 22, 1844. He received his endowment in the Nauvoo temple on May 12, 1844. During the rest of May and June, William again served a mission in the eastern states. He returned to Nauvoo after he received word of the murders of Joseph and Hyrum Smith and supported the Quorum of the Twelve as they took up the reins of leadership following the death of the prophet.

Smith was ordained Presiding Patriarch of the church on May 24, 1845; during the following summer he gave several patriarchal blessings.

William's family life changed drastically during this period. His wife, Caroline, died on May 22, 1845. Shortly afterwards, he took on the responsibilities entailed under the covenant of plural marriage. He married Mary Jane Rollins on June 22, 1845, and later that year was sealed to Mary Ann West, Mary Jones, Priscilla Mogridge, and Sarah and Hannah Libbey.

Smith was dropped as a member of the Quorum of the Twelve and as Patriarch to the church on October 6, 1845; he was excommunicated on October 12 for apostasy. Later that fall

William left on a trip for the eastern states to preach against Brigham Young; he returned to Nauvoo in March 1846.

After his excommunication, William associated with several different apostate LDS factions, including one-year membership (1846-47) with the group established by James J. Strang. In 1847 he established his own church, the Church of Jesus Christ of Latter Day Saints. This group, however, disintegrated within a short period of time. Early in 1860 William was rebaptized into the LDS church by J. J. Butler; however, he subsequently withdrew from the church and, in 1878, joined the Reorganized Church of Jesus Christ of Latter Day Saints.

In the meantime Smith continued to form polygamous relationships, largely with women who had once been associated with the Mormon church. He married Roxie Ann Grant on May 18, 1847; they had two children. Sometime before 1858 he married Eliza Elise; they became the parents of three children. In 1858 Smith moved his extended family to Lee County, Iowa.

Smith died in Osterdock, Clayton County, Iowa, on November 13, 1893 (Cook, *Revelations*, 276-77, 342; *LDSBE*, 1:86-87; and Steven L. Shields, *Divergent Paths of the Restoration*, 4th rev. ed. [Los Angeles, CA: Restoration Research, 1990], 53-55).

3. The date for this meeting is incorrect. It was held February 14, 1835 (see *HC*, 2:180-200; B. H. Roberts, *A Comprehensive History of the Church of Jesus Christ of Latter-day Saints, Century I*, 6 vols. [Provo, UT: Brigham Young University Press, 1965], 1:371-76).

4. D&C 18:9, 26-32, 37-47; compare Wood, 2[1833]:34-39, where the text appears as 15:10-11, 27-36, 42-50. For background, see Cook, *Revelations*, 29-30, 124-25.

5. Whitmer only listed eleven apostles in this manuscript. William Smith's name was left off. This omission may have been deliberate rather than accidental: David Whitmer reflected on what may have been a general bias against William Smith in an 1885 interview with Zenas H. Gurley (Lyndon W. Cook, ed.,

David Whitmer Interviews: A Restoration Witness [Orem, UT: Grandin Book Co., 1991], 157). It may be that John Whitmer shared in this opinion.

6. David W. Patten was born on November 17, 1799, in Vermont, and later settled in Monroe County, Michigan. While he was living in Michigan, he married Phoebe Ann Babcock in 1828.

David was converted to the LDS church by his brother, John. David traveled from Michigan to Fairplay, Indiana, early in 1832 and was baptized on June 15; two days later he was ordained an elder by Elisha Groves. Shortly afterwards David returned to Michigan as a missionary for the Mormon church. In September he moved to Kirtland, Ohio, arriving sometime in October.

The rest of Patten's life was largely occupied by missionary work and other church service. He was ordained a high priest on September 2, 1832, by Hyrum Smith. From October 1832 through February 1833, David filled a mission in Pennsylvania; the following month, March 1833, he left on another mission, this time to the eastern states with Reynolds Cahoon. In New York the pair established several branches of the church. The two returned to Kirtland in the fall of 1833.

After returning, Patten participated in the construction of the Kirtland temple. David was sent to Clay County, Missouri, with William Pratt on December 19, 1833, with letters to church leaders in Missouri from authorities in Kirtland; he remained in Missouri until the arrival of Zion's Camp in June 1834. During the fall of 1834 Patten went to Tennessee on a mission with Warren Parrish.

On February 15, 1835, Patten was ordained an apostle in Kirtland, Ohio, under the hands of David Whitmer, Martin Harris, and Joseph Smith. That summer he accompanied the Quorum of the Twelve on their mission to the eastern states. The next spring, following the quorum's return to Kirtland, Patten participated in the dedication of the Kirtland temple in March 1836. He served a mission to Kentucky and Tennessee that year as well.

Patten and his wife moved to Far West, Missouri, sometime late in 1836. During the spring of 1837 David filled another mission in the eastern states. On February 10, 1838, following the rejection of the presidency of the church in Missouri by the Saints, Patten was called to serve with Thomas B. Marsh as a presidency *pro tem* over the church in Missouri.

David also played a role in the so-called "Mormon War" in Missouri in 1838. He was authorized to lead a body of Caldwell County militia to rescue kidnapped Mormons being held by a mob encamped on the Crooked River in Ray County, Missouri, on October 24, 1838; the next day, during the dawn attack on mob positions, Patten was mortally wounded and died. He was buried in Far West, Missouri, on October 27, 1838; his wife died in Nauvoo on January 5, 1841 (Cook, *Revelations*, 226, 332; *LDSBE*, 1:76-80).

7. Orson Hyde was born on January 8, 1805, in Oxford, New Haven County, Connecticut; by 1817 he had lost both of his parents. Two years later he moved to Ohio, where he became a member of the Methodist church in 1827. About this same time he took up residence with Sidney Rigdon and his family and converted to the Campbellite movement.

Hyde was baptized into the LDS church on October 2, 1831, by Sidney Rigdon, and ordained an elder shortly after. He served a number of missions for the church, starting with a call in January 1832 to serve in the eastern states with Samuel H. Smith. During their eleven-month mission the pair baptized sixty people. Early in 1833 Hyde served a mission with Hyrum Smith in Erie County, Pennsylvania.

Following their return to Kirtland, Hyde continued his activity in church affairs. During 1833 he attended the School of the Prophets. On June 6, 1833, he was called to serve as a clerk to the First Presidency. Later that year he was sent to Missouri with John Gould in an attempt to get the governor of Missouri to redress the grievances of the Saints. They left Kirtland in mid-August and returned on November 25. The following spring Orson returned to Missouri as a member of Zion's Camp.

Hyde assumed family responsibilities as well. He married Marinda Nancy Johnson on September 4, 1834; they had ten children.

On February 15, 1835, Hyde was called and ordained an apostle and a member of the Quorum of the Twelve; that summer he joined the Twelve in serving a mission to the eastern states.

Orson had his problems as well: he was disfellowshipped on August 4, 1835, for "defaming" Sidney Rigdon; however, he was restored to fellowship September 26.

Once restored, Hyde continued his church activities in Kirtland. In March 1836 he attended dedicatory ceremonies of the Kirtland temple; in the winter of 1835-36 he attended the Hebrew School. During the summer he served a mission to Upper Canada. After returning, he was sent to Columbus, Ohio, to seek a corporate charter from the state legislature for a bank in Kirtland; he returned to Kirtland about January 1, 1837, after seeing the Saints' application rejected. In spite of the state's refusal, a financial organization was organized in the city known as the Kirtland Safety Society Anti-Banking Corporation.

8. Heber C. Kimball was born on June 14, 1801, at Sheldon, Franklin County, Vermont. With his family, he moved to West Bloomfield, Ontario County, New York, in 1811. He learned blacksmithing from his father and the potter's trade from his brother Charles.

By 1822 Heber was living in Mendon, New York. He married Vilate Murray in November 1822; they had ten children. Kimball was initiated into Masonry in Victor, New York, in 1823.

Heber was baptized into the Mormon church in April 1832 by Alpheus Gifford and ordained an elder shortly afterwards. He traveled to Kirtland, Ohio, to meet the prophet Joseph Smith that fall; he arrived in November. A year later Kimball moved his family there.

Kimball marched with Zion's Camp during the spring of 1834, returning to Ohio from Missouri on June 20. He arrived in Kirtland on July 26. A month later he had established a pottery in the Kirtland area. During the winter of 1834-35 he attended the School of the Prophets.

Heber was ordained an apostle on February 14, 1835, and filled a mission to the eastern states that summer with the rest of the Quorum of the Twelve. He returned to Kirtland on September 25.

In March 1836 Kimball participated in the dedication of the Kirtland temple. On May 10, 1836, he left for a mission in upstate New York and Vermont, returning to Kirtland on October 2. In January 1837 he became a charter member and stockholder in the Kirtland Safety Society Anti-Banking Corporation.

On June 4, 1837, Heber was called to serve a mission in England with the rest of the apostles. He left Kirtland June 13, 1837, and returned May 22, 1838, having established the gospel in the British Isles and, with the rest of the Twelve, having baptized nearly 1,500 people. Finding the church in the process of moving to Missouri, Kimball packed up his family and left Kirtland; they arrived in Far West on June 25, 1838. After the Saints were expelled from the state, the Kimballs moved to Illinois, settling in Nauvoo during the summer of 1839.

In September 1839, in company with the rest of the Quorum of the Twelve, Kimball returned to the British Isles on another mission. He returned to Nauvoo from England on July 1, 1841. Heber received his endowment on May 4, 1842, and that fall filled a mission in Illinois; he returned in November. On March 11, 1844, he became a member of the Council of Fifty.

In addition to his church activities, Heber was active in civic affairs as well. He was elected to the Nauvoo City Council on October 23, 1841.

Kimball entered the practice of plural marriage in Nauvoo, marrying Sarah Noon in 1842; they became the parents of three children. He married Sarah Ann Whitney in 1846; they had seven children. During 1846-47 he also married Lucy Walker, with whom he had nine children; Prescinda Huntington, with whom he had two children; Clarrisa Cutler, with whom he had one child; Emily Cutler, with whom he had one child; Mary Ellen Abel, with whom he had one child; Ruth Reese, with whom he had three children; Christeen Golden, with whom he had four children; Anna Gheen, with whom he had five children; Amanda Green, with whom he had four children; Harriet Sander, with whom he had three children; Ellen Sanders, with whom he had five children; Frances Swan, with whom he had one child; Martha Knight, with whom he had one child; and Mary Smithies, with whom he had five children.

Heber left Nauvoo again in May 1844 for the eastern states, serving a mission campaigning for the election of Joseph Smith as president of the United States. He returned to Nauvoo on August 6, 1844. Supporting Brigham Young and the rest of the Twelve, Kimball prepared his extended family and the rest of the Saints to leave Illinois. Kimball finally left Nauvoo late in 1846. That year the family reached Winter Quarters, Nebraska, where they remained until 1847.

Kimball entered the Salt Lake Valley with the advance company of pioneers on July 24, 1847; on October 31, 1847, he was back in Winter Quarters. The following May Heber moved his family to the Valley, arriving in September.

On December 27, 1847, Heber was sustained as a counselor to Brigham Young in the First Presidency of the church. He served in that capacity until his death in 1868.

While Kimball was residing in Utah, he again became an active participant in civic and territorial matters. He was elected lieutenant governor of the provisional State of Deseret in 1849 and also served in the territorial legislature.

Heber C. Kimball died June 22, 1868, in Salt Lake City, Utah (Cook, *Revelations*, 263-64, 340; *LDSBE*, I:34-37; Orson F. Whitney, *Life of Heber C. Kimball, An Apostle* [Salt Lake City: Bookcraft, 1974]; and Stanley B. Kimball, *Heber C. Kimball: Mormon Patriarch and Pioneer* [Urbana: University of Illinois Press,

1981]). For a history of the missionary work accomplished in England by the Quorum of the Twelve, see James B. Allen, Ronald K. Esplin, and David J. Whittaker, *Men with a Mission: The Quorum of the Twelve Apostles in the British Isles, 1837-1841* (Salt Lake City: Deseret Book Co., 1992).

9. Luke Johnson was born on November 3, 1807, in Pomfret, Windsor County, Vermont. He was baptized into the Mormon church on May 10, 1831, by Joseph Smith; Christian Whitmer ordained Johnson a priest shortly afterwards. Sometime before October he was ordained an elder. During 1831 Johnson also filled a mission for the church with Robert Rathburn in southern Ohio and Pittsburgh, Pennsylvania. In southern Ohio they joined with Sidney Rigdon, preaching the gospel in the New Portage, Ohio, area, and together baptized about fifty people.

Luke was ordained a high priest on October 25, 1831. During 1832-33 he filled a mission to Virginia and Kentucky with Seymour Brunson and Hazen Aldrich; they baptized more than a hundred people.

Johnson married Susan H. Poteet on November 1, 1833; they became the parents of six children.

On February 17, 1834, Johnson was called to serve as a high councilor in Kirtland. That spring and summer he traveled to Missouri with Zion's Camp.

Luke Johnson was ordained an apostle and a member of the original Quorum of the Twelve on February 15, 1835; that summer he served a mission in the eastern states with the rest of the quorum, returning to Kirtland in September. During the winter of 1835-36 Luke attended the Hebrew School in Kirtland and participated in the dedication of the Kirtland temple in March 1836. Johnson later served a mission in New York and Upper Canada, returning to Kirtland that fall.

Johnson was a charter member and a stockholder in the Kirtland Safety Society Anti-Banking Corporation in January 1837. Following the collapse of the bank that year, Johnson became alienated from Joseph Smith, filing charges against the prophet in May for "speaking reproachfully against the brethren." Johnson was disfellowshipped on September 3, 1837, and formally excommunicated from the church in December 1838.

After leaving the LDS church, Johnson taught school in Cabell County, Virginia, as well as studying medicine. Following completion of his studies, Johnson returned to Kirtland, where he became a practicing physician.

Luke returned to the Mormon church on March 8, 1846, being baptized in Nauvoo, Illinois, by Orson Hyde. In March 1847 he married America Morgan Clark, with whom he had eight children. The family arrived in the Salt Lake Valley in July 1847.

Johnson received his endowment on April 1, 1854, and subsequently settled in St. John, Tooele County, Utah, where he was called to serve as a bishop.

Luke Johnson died in the home of his brother-in-law, Orson Hyde, in Salt Lake City, Utah, on December 9, 1861 (Cook, *Revelations*, 110-11, 146; *LDSBE*, 1:85-86).

10. Lyman E. Johnson was born on October 24, 1811, in Pomfret, Windsor County, Vermont. About 1820 his family moved to Hiram, Ohio. Lyman was baptized a Mormon in February 1831 by Sidney Rigdon and ordained an elder on October 25, 1831, by Oliver Cowdery. On November 1, Johnson was ordained a high priest.

Johnson was called to serve a mission with Orson Pratt on January 25, 1832; the pair left for the eastern states on February 3, preaching in Pennsylvania, New York, New Jersey, Vermont, New Hampshire, Connecticut, and Massachusetts. They returned to Kirtland in February 1833, having baptized more than a hundred people.

Lyman served several other missions in the eastern states as well. He left Kirtland with Orson Pratt on March 26, 1833, and returned on September 28, having baptized fifty people. Johnson left again with Pratt, this time on November 27, 1833, and returned to Kirtland on February 13, 1834. He was also called to fill a mission in Upper Canada with Milton Holmes on February 20, 1834.

Johnson marched to Missouri with Zion's Camp in 1834. On February 14, 1835, he was ordained an apostle.

Sometime before 1836 he married Sarah Lang; they had two children.

Lyman was a charter member of the Kirtland Safety Society Anti-Banking Corporation in January 1837; after the bank collapsed shortly afterwards in the Panic of 1837, he claimed to have lost $6,000. In May, Johnson charged Joseph Smith with slander and lying. On September 3 he was temporarily disfellowshipped. He moved to Far West, Missouri, late in 1837, where he associated with LDS dissenters. Johnson was excommunicated for apostasy on April 13, 1838, in Far West.

By 1842 the family had moved to Iowa, where Lyman practiced law in Davenport and Keokuk.

Lyman Johnson died on December 20, 1856, at Prairie du Chien, Wisconsin, having drowned in the Mississippi River (Cook, *Revelations*, 111, 146; *LDSBE*, 1:91-92).

11. Brigham Young was on born June 1, 1801, in Whittingham, Windham County, Vermont. He moved with his family to Sherburne, New York, in 1804, and from there to Auburn, New York, in 1813. Around 1822 Young joined the Methodist church. He married Miriam Works in Aurilius, New York, on October 8, 1824; they had two children. Brigham was employed as a carpenter, joiner, painter, and glazier. In 1829 the family moved to Mendon, New York.

Brigham first saw the Book of Mormon in the spring of 1830. He was baptized on April 14, 1832, by Eleazer Miller and ordained an elder, by his own account, "before the shirt was dry on my back."

Young's first wife, Miriam, died on September 8, 1832. The following October and November, Brigham traveled to Kirtland, Ohio, to meet Joseph Smith. In December he filled a mission to Upper Canada, the first of what was to become many. After a short return to Mendon, New York, in February 1833, he went on a second mission to Upper Canada which lasted from April to August 1833. In September, Young moved to Kirtland.

On February 18, 1834, Brigham married Mary Ann Angell; they had six children. During the spring and summer of 1834 he participated in the march of Zion's Camp to Missouri. After returning to Kirtland, he assisted in the construction of the Kirtland temple.

Brigham Young was ordained an apostle on February 14, 1835, and left for a mission to the eastern states with the rest of the Quorum of the Twelve in May. He returned to Kirtland in September 1835.

During the fall and winter of 1835-36 Young attended the Hebrew School in Kirtland. In March 1836 he participated in the dedication of the Kirtland temple.

Brigham became a charter member and stockholder in the Kirtland Safety Society Anti-Banking Corporation in January 1837. Unlike many others, however—including five members of the Quorum of the Twelve—he did not blame the bank's failure on the prophet. Young remained one of the steadiest and most trusted friends Joseph Smith had during his lifetime.

Young filled several more missions for the church before the Saints left Ohio for Missouri. With Willard Richards, he served a mission in the eastern states which lasted from March to June 1837, and then another mission to New York and Massachusetts which went from June through August.

Brigham moved his family to Missouri on December 22, 1837, arriving in the town of Far West on March 14, 1838. Expelled from the state with the rest of the Saints late that year, Young organized the evacuation of the Mormons from Missouri and the move to Illinois.

Young and his family located temporarily in Quincy, Illinois, in February 1839, following their move from Missouri, and moved to Montrose, Iowa, in May.

Filling a call given to the Quorum of the Twelve, Young left Nauvoo on a mission to the British Isles on September 14, 1839, arriving on April 6, 1840. While the Twelve were serving in England, a reorganization of the Quorum by Joseph Smith caused Brigham Young to be called to serve as president; this move came on January 19, 1841. Brigham left Britain with most of the rest of the Twelve on April 21, 1841, and returned to Nauvo on July 1.

Young was active in Nauvoo civic affairs as well. He was elected a member of the Nauvoo City Council on September 4, 1841. On April 7, 1842, he became a Mason. On March 11, 1844, he attended his first meeting of the Council of the Fifty. He was elected lieutenant general of the Nauvoo Legion on August 31, 1844—a position that Joseph Smith had filled before his death.

Young received his endowment on May 4, 1842; on June 15 he married his first plural wife, Lucy Ann Decker. They became the parents of seven children. He took on further family responsibilities over the years, marrying Harriet E. Cook in 1843; Clarissa Decker in 1844, with whom he had five children; Clarissa Ross in 1844, with whom he had four children; Emily Dow Partridge in 1844, with whom he had seven children; Louisa Beman in 1846, with whom he had five children; Margaret Maria Alley in 1846, with whom he had two children; Emmeline Free in 1846, with whom he had ten children; Margaret Pierce in 1846, with whom he had one child; Zina D. Huntington in 1846, with whom he had one child; Lucy Bigelow in 1847, with whom he had three children; Eliza Burgess in 1852, with whom he had one child; Harriet Barney in 1856, with whom he had one child; Mary Van Cott in 1865, with whom he had one child.

Brigham left again on a mission to the eastern states, this time to collect funds from the Saints for the Nauvoo House and Nauvoo temple; he left in July and returned in September 1843. He went on another mission east to campaign for Joseph Smith's candidacy as president of the United States, leaving on May 21, 1844, and returning on August 6, 1844.

In the confused days that followed the prophet's death,

Brigham asserted the right of the Quorum of the Twelve to lead the church. Many people who listened to him speak during the meetings that were called for August 7 later claimed they saw him transfigured into the prophet, evidence that the mantle of leadership was now his as president of the Quorum of the Twelve. The majority of the Saints voted to sustain Young and the rest of the Quorum as the leaders of the church.

As president of the Twelve, Young directed the preparations for the march West and supervised the exodus from Nauvoo. He left Nauvoo on February 15, 1846; that fall he stopped the trains and established the town of Winter Quarters on the banks of the Missouri River in what is now Nebraska.

Young left Winter Quarters for the Rocky Mountains on April 14, 1847; his advance party arrived in the Salt Lake Valley on July 24, 1847. Leaving most of the company behind to attend to plowing and planting, Young returned to Winter Quarters on August 18. He was ordained president of the church and the First Presidency was reorganized on December 5, 1847, at Kanesville, Iowa. Young set out on his return to the Salt Lake Valley on May 26, 1848, arriving on September 20.

Brigham was elected governor of the provisional State of Deseret on March 12, 1849. He was appointed governor of the officially organized Territory of Utah by President Millard Fillmore on September 20, 1850. He also served as federal Indian Superintendent for the territory.

During the rest of his life, Brigham founded hundreds of settlements which stretched from Canada to Mexico and west into Nevada and California, organizing local church units, calling missionaries, and related activities. He was actively involved in the economic life of Utah, building local railroad lines and lobbying successfully for the final stretches of the new intercontinental railroad and the overland telegraph to be completed in the Territory.

Brigham Young died in Salt Lake City on August 29, 1877 (Cook, *Revelations*, 279-81, 343; *LDSBE*, 1:8-14; Leonard J. Arrington, *Brigham Young: American Moses* [New York: Alfred A.

Knopf, 1985]; Andrew F. Ehat, "Joseph Smith's Introduction of Temple Ordinances and the 1844 Mormon Succession Question," M.A. thesis, Brigham Young University, 1982; Ronald K. Esplin, "The Emergence of Brigham Young and the Twelve to Mormon Leadership, 1830-1841," Ph.D. diss., Brigham Young University, 1981; and "Joseph, Brigham and the Twelve: A Succession of Continuity," *Brigham Young University Studies* 21 [Summer 1981]: 301-41).

12. John F. Boynton was born on September 20, 1811, in Bradford, Essex County, Massachusetts. He was baptized in September 1832 in Kirtland, Ohio, by Joseph Smith and ordained an elder by Sidney Rigdon. He filled a mission that year with Zebedee Coltrin in Pennsylvania and a second one in Maine that lasted from 1833 through 1834.

On February 15, 1835, Boynton was ordained an apostle and a member of the original Quorum of the Twelve; shortly afterwards he left with the rest of the Twelve on their mission to the eastern states. John married Susan Lowell on January 20, 1836.

Boynton entered the mercantile business with Lyman E. Johnson, a trade he maintained until after he apostatized and was disfellowshipped from the Quorum of the Twelve on September 3, 1837, in Kirtland, another spiritual victim of the Kirtland Safety Society Anti-Banking Corporation failure. The following Sunday he made a complete confession and was forgiven, but since his subsequent actions showed he had not truly repented of his sins, he was formally excommunicated from the church shortly afterwards.

After leaving the church, Boynton associated briefly with Warren Parrish and several other excommunicated church leaders in establishing a group known as the Church of Christ. After the group disintegrated, he settled in Syracuse, New York, becoming a noted scientist and inventor. He never again became a member of any other religious group.

John F. Boynton died on October 20, 1890, in Syracuse, New York (*LDSBE*, 1:91; Steven L. Shields, *Divergent Paths of the*

Restoration 4th rev. ed. [Los Angeles, CA: Restoration Research, 1990], 22-23).

13. Zebedee Coltrin was born on September 7, 1804, in Ovid, Seneca County, New York; in 1814 he accompanied his family when they moved to Strongsville, Cuyahoga County, Ohio. Sometime before 1828, Coltrin married Julia Ann Jennings; they had five children, all of whom died in infancy.

Zebedee was baptized on January 9, 1831, by Solomon Hancock and confirmed a member of the church on January 19 by Lyman Wight. Two days later he was ordained an elder by John Whitmer.

Coltrin was called to travel to Missouri with Levi W. Hancock on June 6, 1831. On the way there, the two stopped and preached in several locations. In Winchester, Indiana, they baptized a number of people and established a large branch of the church there. Zebedee returned to Kirtland from Missouri on June 15, 1832; on July 17 he was ordained a high priest.

Coltrin was one of the original students in the School of the Prophets when it opened in January 1833. On July 20, 1834, he was called on a mission to Upper Canada; that spring he marched to Missouri with Zion's Camp.

Coltrin was ordained a member of the First Quorum of the Seventy on February 28, 1835; on March 1 he was ordained one of the Seven Presidents of the Seventy. He was released from the presidency of the quorum on April 6, 1837.

In 1836 Zebedee went back to class at the School of the Prophets in Kirtland. In March he participated in the dedication of the Kirtland temple. Coltrin was also a stockholder in the Kirtland Safety Society Anti-Banking Corporation in 1837.

Coltrin settled his family in Nauvoo in 1839. Shortly afterwards, he returned to Kirtland, where, on May 22, 1841, he was called to serve in the Kirtland Stake presidency. By 1842, after the Kirtland Stake had been formally dissolved, he was back in Nauvoo.

Zebedee left Nauvoo for the eastern states to campaign for

Joseph Smith's presidential candidacy in April 1844; he returned to Nauvoo after receiving word of the prophet's death. On December 22, 1845, he received his endowment in the Nauvoo temple.

Coltrin left Illinois with the rest of the Saints in 1846. After settling temporarily in Winter Quarters, he arrived in the Salt Lake Valley with the advance company on July 24, 1847. He returned to Winter Quarters shortly afterwards and brought his family back to the valley with him; they arrived in 1851. In 1852 Coltrin was called to settle in Spanish Fork, Utah. On May 31, 1873, he was ordained a patriarch by John Taylor.

Sometime during this period he married Mary Lott; they had eight children.

Zebedee Coltrin died in Spanish Fork, Utah County, Utah, on July 21, 1887 (Cook, *Revelations*, 75-76, 138; *LDSBE*, 1:190).

14. Sylvester Smith, no known relation to Joseph Smith, was born about 1805. In 1830 the census listed him as a resident of Amherst, Lorain County, Ohio. He was baptized into the Mormon church and ordained an elder sometime before June 1831. Sylvester was ordained a high priest on October 25, 1831, by Oliver Cowdery.

Smith was called to preach with Gideon Carter on January 25, 1832. The two traveled together from Ohio to Vermont, preaching along the way. They left the Kirtland area on April 5, 1832, and returned in August, having baptized several converts.

Sylvester assisted in laying the foundation stones for the Kirtland temple on July 23, 1833; in 1834 he marched to Missouri with Zion's Camp.

Proving to be a contentious person during the march of the Camp, he was tried in August 1834 for "traducing" the character of Joseph Smith; upon confession of his sins, he was subsequently forgiven.

Smith was appointed a member of the Kirtland high council on February 17, 1835; on February 28 he was ordained a Seventy. He was ordained to the presidency of the Seventy on

March 1. During August and September he served as clerk for the high council, and on January 25, 1836, he was called as an acting scribe for Joseph Smith.

Sylvester attended the School of the Prophets and later the Hebrew School in Kirtland. In January 1836 he attended the solemn assembly called to meet in Kirtland. In March he participated in the dedication of the Kirtland temple.

Smith was released from the Kirtland high council on January 13, 1836, and from the presidency of the Seventy on April 6, 1837.

Smith was also a charter member and stockholder in the Kirtland Safety Society Anti-Banking Corporation in January 1837. He became a vocal opponent of Joseph Smith following the failure of the bank, and by 1838 he had left the church (Cook, *Revelations*, 156, 311; *LDSBE*, 1:191).

15. Not much is known about Leonard Rich. His name is first mentioned in the history of Joseph Smith in connection with a council of high priests and elders held in Kirtland, Ohio, on February 12, 1834. In this meeting he was tried for transgressing the Word of Wisdom and for "selling the revelations at an extortionary price while journeying east with Father Lyons." Rich confessed his sins and the council forgave him upon his promise to reform his life.

In 1834 Leonard marched to Missouri with Zion's Camp and, on February 28, 1835, was ordained to the First Quorum of the Seventy; shortly afterwards he was called into the presidency of the quorum and took an active part in the public affairs of the church for some time. Having previously been ordained a high priest, Rich was released from the Seventy and joined the high priest's quorum.

In September 1837 Rich's actions were again called into question; a letter written by the prophet simply says, "Leonard Rich and others have been in transgression, but we hope they may be humble, and ere long make satisfaction to the Church; otherwise they cannot retain their standing." The outcome is not known (*LDSBE*, 1:189-90).

16. Hazen Aldrich's birthdate and birthplace are not known. He was ordained a high priest sometime before 1834.

Aldrich marched to Missouri with Zion's Camp during the spring and summer of 1834. On February 28, 1835, he was ordained a member of the First Quorum of the Seventy and called into the quorum presidency shortly afterwards. Since he was a high priest, however, on April 6, 1837, he was released from the presidency and rejoined the high priest's quorum.

During the great schism which occurred in the church following the failure of the Kirtland Safety Society Anti-Banking Corporation in 1837, Aldrich became alienated from the church and apostatized. He subsequently joined the Brewster movement and published a paper in Kirtland called *The Olive Branch*; the first issue came off the presses in August 1848.

Aldrich became a leader in the Brewster movement and finally emigrated to California, where he died (*LDSBE*, 1:186-87; for information on the Brewsterites and Aldrich's involvement with them, see Shields, *Divergent Paths of the Restoration*, 55-56).

17. Joseph Young, an older brother of Brigham Young, was born on April 7, 1797, in Hopkinton, Middlesex County, Massachusetts. He joined the Methodists while still a young man and eventually became a preacher.

Joseph was introduced to Mormonism in 1832 by his brother, Brigham. Joseph Young was baptized on April 6, 1832, by Daniel Bowen in Columbia, Pennsylvania, and ordained an elder a few days later. Joseph left on a mission for the LDS church shortly afterwards, spending several months in New York and then going on to Canada with his brother Phineas, Eleazer Miller, and several others. While they were in Canada, they established two small branches. The group returned to New York four months later.

In company with Brigham Young and Heber C. Kimball, Joseph moved his family to Kirtland, Ohio. From here he was called to go on another mission to Canada with Brigham during the winter of 1832-33. While there they established a branch of about twenty members. They were gone about six weeks and baptized approximately forty people.

Joseph Young married Jane Adeline Bicknell on February 18, 1834; they had eleven children.

Joseph marched to Missouri with Zion's Camp during the spring and summer of 1834, returning to Kirtland that fall. On February 28, 1835, he was ordained a member of the First Quorum of the Seventy. In 1835 he filled another mission for the church, this time to the states of New York and Massachusetts. His companion for this mission was Burr Riggs.

In 1836 Joseph participated in the dedication of the Kirtland temple and received the related ordinances. He was then called on another mission to the eastern states, this time in company with his brother, Brigham. Their specific calling was to visit their relatives and friends that still resided there and teach them the gospel. The pair was gone several months. As a result of their efforts, many of their relatives joined the church.

On July 6, 1838, Joseph Young moved his family to Missouri, arriving at the town of Haun's Mill on October 28. Two days later, on October 30, 1838, Young witnessed the Massacre of Haun's Mill. Miraculously, he survived.

During the winter of 1838-39, and the expulsion of the Mormons from Missouri, the Youngs moved to Quincy, Illinois, settling there in May 1839. That season Joseph farmed some land he had purchased; in the spring of 1840 the family relocated in Nauvoo. Here Joseph became a painter and a glazier; he also continued to be active in the affairs of his quorum.

Young was called on a mission to Ohio to stump for the presidency of Joseph Smith in the spring of 1844. He returned to Nauvoo after receiving news of the prophet's death.

Sustaining the Twelve in their leadership of the church, Young moved his family from Nauvoo to the West in 1846. The family settled temporarily at Carterville, Iowa, and then at Winter Quarters until 1850, when they finally arrived in the Salt Lake Valley.

After reaching Utah, Joseph continued to travel the territory and preach extensively; in 1870 he filled a mission in the British Isles.

Joseph Young died in Salt Lake City, Utah, on July 16, 1881 (*LDSBE*, 1:187-88).

18. Levi Hancock was born on April 7, 1803, in Old Springfield, Hampden County, Massachusetts. In 1805 the family moved to Ontario County, New York; about 1820 they were in Chagrin, Ohio. Levi became a cabinetmaker by profession and a good musician.

Hancock was baptized into the Mormon church by Parley P. Pratt in November 1830 and ordained an elder shortly thereafter by Oliver Cowdery.

In June 1831 Levi was called to travel to Jackson County, Missouri, with Zebedee Coltrin, teaching the gospel as they went. They had a great deal of success, establishing a large branch of the church in Winchester, Indiana.

In 1833 Hancock married Clarissa Reed; they became the parents of eight children.

Levi traveled to Missouri with Zion's Camp in 1834. On February 28, 1835, he was ordained a Seventy and called to the presidency of the First Quorum of the Seventy shortly afterwards, a position he held until his death.

In 1838 Hancock moved his family to Missouri; after the expulsion of the Saints from the state in 1838-39, he relocated in Nauvoo.

While in Nauvoo, Levi served in the Nauvoo Legion and was probably ordained a member of the Council of Fifty on April 18, 1844. Hancock received his endowment in the Nauvoo temple on December 12, 1845.

In 1846 Hancock and his family left Illinois for the West. En route he served as a member of the Mormon Battalion from July 1846 until July 1847. The Hancocks arrived in the Salt Lake Valley in October 1847.

Hancock also faithfully followed the practice of plural marriage. Sometime before 1849 he married Emily Melissa Richey;

they had three children. On July 19, 1857, he married Anne Tew; they had seven children. He also married Elizabeth Woodville Hovey and Mary Mogen, but the dates are unknown; no children are known to have been born from these unions.

Levi moved to Payson, Utah, and lived there from 1850 to 1851. In September 1851 he was elected as a representative to the territorial assembly from Utah County.

The Hancocks assisted in the settling of Manti, Sanpete County, Utah, in 1852. While residing there, Levi was again elected to the territorial assembly.

Levi was called to preach the gospel along the Wasatch Front as a "home missionary" in October 1852; by 1855 he was back in Payson. In 1862 the family relocated again, this time back to Salt Lake City.

Hancock was called to go on a cotton mission in November 1862; by 1863 he was back in Salt Lake City. About 1866 the family moved to southern Utah, there assisting in settling Harrisburg, Leeds, and Washington. In 1872 Levi was ordained a patriarch.

Levi Hancock died on June 10, 1882, in Washington, Washington County, Utah (Cook, *Revelations*, 76-77, 139; *LDSBE*, 1:188-89).

19. See *HC*, 2:181-200, 201-208.

Chapter 16
Mummies and Murmurings

CHAPTER 16

In June 1835 a man by the name of Hewet came from England, and presented to a counsel the following Letter [from Thomas Shaw of the Barnsley Independent Church] as follows.

Dear brethren in the Lord.

At a counsel of the Pastors of our church, held March 28, 1835, upon the propriety of the Reverend John Hewet visiting you—It was resolved and approved, that as he had an anxious desire to go to America, to see the things spoken of in one of your papers, brought here by a Merchant from New York, he should have as he desired, the sanction of the counsel and if it pleased the Lord his approval.

The Lord has seen our joy and gladness to hear that he was raising up a people, for himself in that part of the New World as well as here—O may our faith increase, that he may have Evangelists, apostles and Prophets, filled with the power of the Spirit, and performing his will in destroying the work of darkness.

The Rev. Mr. Hewet was professer of Mathematics in Rotherdam Independent [p. 75] Seminary, and four years Pastor in Barnsley Independent Church, the[n] commenced preaching the doctrine we taught, about two years sinc, and was excommunicated, many of his flock followed him, so that eventually he was installed in the same church, and the Lord['s] work prospered. As he is a living Epistle, you will have. if all be well, a full explanation, Ma[n]y will follow should he approve of the country &c. who will helps the cause because the Lord the Lord has favored them with this worlds goods

We had an utterance during our meeting which caused us to sing for Joy. The Lord was pleased with our brothers holy determination to see you, and we understand that persecution had been great among you or would be—But we were commanded not to fear for he would be with us,—Praise the Lord. The time is at hand when distance shall be no barrier between us, but when on the wings of love—Jehovahs messengers shall be communicated by his Saints.

The Lord bless our brother. And may he prove a blessing to you—be not afraid of our enemies, they shall unless they repent, be cast down by the Lord of hosts,—The workers of iniquity have been used by the prince of darkness, to play the counterfeit, but dicernment has been given, that they were immediately put to shame by being detected, so that the flock never suffered, as yet by them. Grace mercy and Peace, be with you from God our Father, and from the Spirit Jesus Christ our Lord Amen.

       I am
              dear sir
                   your brother
                        in the gospel,
Barnsley England April 21, 1835. Thomas Shaw

This Mr. Hewet did not obey the gospel. neither would he investigate the matter. Thus ended the mission of Mr. Hewet.[1]

About the first of July 1835 there came a man having four Egyptian Mummies exhibiting them for curiosities, which was a wonder indeed having also some records connected with them which were found deposited with the Mummies, but there being no one skilled in the Egyptian language therefore [he] could not translate the record, after this exhibition Joseph the Seer saw these Record[s] and by the revelation of Jesus Christ could translate these records, which gave an account of our forefathers, ~~even abraham~~ Much of which was written by Joseph of Egypt who was sold by his brethren Which when all translated will be a pleasing history and of great value to the saints.[2]

And it came to pass while we were yet in the East, there came some letters to the Presidency respecting the Presidency of the Elders of Zion, there being some difficulty concerning the matter among them.

Therefore the following letter was written to Zion.

[p. 77]

Kirtland August 31, 1835.

The Presiden[c]y of Kirtland and Zion say that the Lord has manifested by revelation of his spirit: that the high preeist, teachers, Priests and deacons, or in other words all the officers in the land of Clay Co. Mo. belonging to the church are more or less in transgression, because they have not enjoyed the Spirit of God sufficiently to be able to comprehend their duties respecting themselves, and the welfare of Zion. Thereby having been left to act, in a manner that is detrimental to the interest, and also a hindrance, to the redemption of Zion.

Now if they will be wise, they will humble themselves in a peculiar manner that God may open the eyes of their understanding. It will be clearly manifest that the design and purposes of the Almighty; are with regard to them and the children of Zion; that they should let the high counsel which is appointed of God, and ordained for that purpose, <make and> regulate all the affairs of Zion: and that it is the will of God, that her children should stand still, and see the salvation of her redemption; and the officers of the church should go forth, inasmuch as they can leave their families in comfortable circumstances; and gather up the saints, even the strength of the Lords house. And those who cannot go forth consistently with the will of God their circumstances preventing them; remain in deep humility: and in as much, [as] they do anything [p. 78] [they should] confine themselves to teaching the first principles of the Gospel: not endeavoring to institute regulations or laws for Zion, without having been appointed of God.

Now we see there is no need of ordaining in Zion, or appointing any more officers: but let all those that are ordained magnify themselves before the Lord: by going into the vineyard and cleansing their garments from the blood of this generation. It is one thing to be ordained to preach the gospel, and to push the people together to Zion, and it is another thing to be annointed to lay the foundation and build up the City of Zion, and execute her laws. Therefore it is certain that many of the Elders have come under great condemnation, in endeavoring to steady the ark of God. in a place when they have not been sent.

The high counsel and bishops court have been established to do the business of Zion, and her children are not bound to acknowledge any of those who feel disposed to run to Zion and set themselves to be their rulers. Let not her children be duped in this way, but let them prove those who say they are apostles and are not.

The Elders have no right to regulate Zion, but they have a

right to preach the gospel. They will all do well to repent and humble themselves, and all the church, and also we ourselves receive the admonition and so now endeavor and pray to this end. [p. 79] When the children of Zion are strangers in a strange land their harps must be hung upon the willows: and they cannot sing the songs of Zion: but should mourn and not dance. Therefore brethren, it remains for all such to be exercised with prayer, and continual supplication, until Zion is redeemed. We realize the situation that all the brethren and sisters must be in, being deprived of their spiritual privileges, which are enjoyed by those who sit in heavenly places in Christ Jesus; where there are no mobs to rise up and bind their consciences. Nevertheless, it is wisdom that the church should make but little or no stir in that region, and cause as little excitement as possible and endure their afflictions patiently until the time appointed—and the Governor of Mo. fulfils his promise in setting the church over upon their own lands. We would suggest an idea that it would be wisdom for all the members of the church on the return of the Bishop [Edward Partridge], to make known to him their names places of residence, &c. that it may be known where they all are when the Governor shall give directions for you to be set over on your lands[.]

Again it is the will of the Lord, that the church should attend to their communion on the sabbath day, and let them remember the commandment which says, "Talk not of Judgment" we are commanded not to give the childrens bread unto the dogs: neither cast our pearls before [p. 80] swine, least they trample them under their feet, and turn again and rend you. Therefore—let us be wise in all things, and keep all the commandments of God, that our salvation may be sure: having our armour ready and prepared against the time appointed; and having on the whole armour of righteousness, we may be able to stand in that trying day. We say also that if there are any doors open for the Elders to preach the first principles of the gospel: let them not keep silence: rail not against the sects, neither talk against their tenets. But preach Christ and him crucified. love to God, and love to man, observing always to make mention of our republican principles, thereby if possible, we may allay the prejudice of the people, be meek and lowly of heart, and the Lord God of our fathers shall be with you for evermore.

Amen.

Sanctioned and signed by the Presidents

       Joseph Smith Jr.

       Oliver Cowdery

       Sidney Rigdon

       F. G. Williams

       W. W. Phelps

       John Whitmer.

P.S. Br Hezekiah Peck

We remember your family, with all the first families of the church, who first embraced the truth, we remember your losses and sorrows, our first ties are not broken, we [p. 81] participate with you in the evil as well as the good, in the sorrows as well as the Joys, our union we trust is stronger than death, and shall never be severed. Remember us unto all who believe in the fulness of the gospel of our Lord and Saviour Jesus Christ. We hereby authorize you Hezekiah Peck, our beloved brother to read this epistle and communicate it unto all the brotherhood in all that region of country. Dictated by me your unworthy brother, and fellow laborer in the testimony of the book of Mormon. Signed by my own hand in the token of the everlasting covenant.

Joseph Smith Jr.

NOTES

1. See *HC*, 2:230-34. Here it is recorded that upon his failure to return and upon discovery that Hewitt and his wife had moved on to Fairport, Ohio, Oliver Cowdery was sent by the First Presidency to the Reverend Hewitt, inviting him to continue his investigations. According to the history:

> Elder Cowdery immediately repaired to Fairport, and on the day following reported to the Council that Mr. Hewitt was not in the place: that he left their letter with Mrs. Hewitt, who informed him that her "husband had frequently spoken of his wish to become further acquainted with the people whom he had come out from Europe to see." But the next we heard of the Reverend John Hewitt was that he had opened a school in Painsville, Ohio (*HC*, 2:233).

2. The subject of the mummies, the existence of the scrolls, and the accuracy of Joseph Smith's translation which now appears in the Book of Abraham in the Pearl of Great Price have been the subject of controversy for many years. Among the most helpful studies are H. Donl Peterson, *The Pearl of Great Price: A History and Commentary* (Salt Lake City: Deseret Book Co., 1987), 3-24, 36-55; *The Story of the Book of Abraham* (Salt Lake City: Deseret Book Co., 1995); and "Antonio Lebolo: Excavator of the Book of Abraham," *Brigham Young University Studies* 31 (Summer 1991): 5-29; and Jay Todd, *The Saga of the Book of Abraham* (Salt Lake City: Deseret Book Co., 1969); Michael Dennis Rhodes, "A Translation and Commentary of the Joseph Smith Hypocephalus," *Brigham Young University Studies* 17 (Spring 1977): 259-74; Christopher C. Lund, "A Letter Regarding the Acquisition of the Book of Abraham," *Brigham Young University Studies* 20 (Summer 1980): 402-403; and James R. Clark, *The Story of*

the *Pearl of Great Price* (Salt Lake City: Bookcraft, 1955), 56-186. Somewhat polemical, but still useful, are Hyrum L. Andrus, *Doctrinal Commentary on the Pearl of Great Price* (Salt Lake City: Deseret Book Co., 1967), 11-28; George Reynolds and Janne M. Sjodahl, *Commentary on the Pearl of Great Price* (Salt Lake City: Deseret Book Co., 1965), 238-85; and Milton R. Hunter, *Pearl of Great Price Commentary* (Salt Lake City: Bookcraft, 1951), 6-40. See also Edward H. Ashment, "The Book of Abraham Facsimiles: A Reappraisal," *Sunstone* 4 (Dec. 1979): 33-48; and Karl C. Sandberg, "Knowing Brother Joseph Again: The Book of Abraham and Joseph Smith as Translator," *Dialogue: A Journal of Mormon Thought* 22 (Winter 1989): 17-37.

[Handwritten annotation: What a pathetic source offering. He entirely ignores the writings in LDS journals which do not affirm the Book of Abraham]

Chapter 17

Anointings

CHAPTER 17

And it came to pass on the 24 day of Sept 1835, on which day we met in course at the house of J. Smith Jr. the Seer, where we according to a previous commandment given, appointed David Whitmer Capt of the Lords host and Prs. F. G. Williams and Sidney Rigdon his assistants. And Pres. W. W. Phelps[,] myself[,] and John Corrill as an assistant quorum, and Joseph Smith Jr. the seer to stand at the head and be assisted by Hyrum Smith and Oliver Cowdry. This much for the war department by revelation.[1]

October 18, 1835. Sabbath
This day assembled in the house of the Lord as usual and the spirit of the [p. 82] Lord decended upon J. Smith Jr. the seer and he prophesied: saying the Lord has showed to me this day by the Spirit of Revelation that the distress, and sickness that has heretofore prevailed among the children of Zion will be mitigated from this time forth.
And it came to pass that some of the first Elders or

President of the church received a Prophetic blessing by revelation through the mean prepared in the last days to receive the word of the Lord. J. Smith. Jr. Therefore Joseph dictated blessings for himself[,] Hyrum Smith, Sidney Rigdon, F. G. Williams, Oliver Cowdery, David Whitmer, W. W. Phelps and myself. As you will find recorded in the Patriarchal blessing Book in Kirtland[,] Ohio—Book A. Pages.—[2]

On the 6th day of Jan. 1836.
The Elders from Zion who were at Kirtland Ohio met, to fill vacancies which hapened in the high Counsel in Zion in consequence ~~of disease and death and~~ filling other stations
Wherefore appointed
E. H. Graves   instead of P. P. Pratt
Jesse Hitchcock   - -   W. E. Mc Lellin
G. M. Hinkle   - -   Orson Pratt
Elias Higbee   - -   T. B. Marsh

The Hebrew school commenced[.]
Jan 4, 1836.
Taught by J. Si<e>xeus.
The first Elders attended this school.
[p. 83] Now the time drew near when the Lord would endow his servants, and before he could do this we must perform all the ordinances that are instituted in his house there was one ordinance Viz. the washing of feet that we had not as yet observed, but did perform it according to Revelation, which ordinance belongs only to ordained members and not the whole church.
For Particulars read the private history of Joseph the Seer.[3]
After the washing of feet came the Annointing with holy oil, which was performed by Joseph Smith seignor, among the

Presidents then the Presidents of each quorum proced[ed] to annoint the members thereof - in their proper time and place.

On the 11, March 1836

Held a counsel in which Edward Partridge[,] I. Morly, John Corrill[,] and W. W. Phelps were appointed wise men and were sent to Mo. with some money [to] purchase land for the saints—to seek a place for them &c.

NOTES

1. The account of this meeting recorded in *HC*, 2:281-82, reads:

> The High Council met at my house on the 24th to take into consideration the redemption of Zion. And it was the voice of the Spirit of the Lord that we petition the Governor, that is, those who have been driven out, shall petition to be set back on their own lands next spring, and that we go next season, to live or die on our own lands, which we have purchased in Jackson County, Missouri. We truly had a good time, and covenanted to struggle for this thing, until death shall dissolve the union; and if one falls, that the remainder be not discouraged, but pursue this object until it be accomplished; which may God grant unto us in the name of Jesus Christ our Lord. Also, this day drew up a subscription for enrolling the names of those who are willing to go up to Missouri next spring and settle; and I ask God in the name of Jesus that we may obtain eight hundred or one thousand emigrants.

Whitmer's references to "Capt of the Lord's host" and "war department" suggest a more militant emphasis.

2. Patriarchal blessings are prophetic utterances pronounced on individual members of the church by ordained patriarchs and were recorded in special patriarchal blessings books. These are currently housed in archives, Historical Department, Church of Jesus Christ of Latter-day Saints, Salt Lake City, Utah, and

access to them is currently restricted.

3. For examples, see *HC*, 1:323-24, 2:429-32, and 2:475-80. However, none of these dates corresponds to the one given here by Whitmer: the first incident occurred on January 23, 1833; the second on March 29, 1836, instead of January 4, as Whitmer recorded here; and the third on February 1, 1837.

Chapter 18

The House of the Lord

CHAPTER 18.

Kirtland March 27, 1836.

Preives [previous] notice having been given, the Church of Latter day Saints met in the house of the Lord &c.

See Mes[senger] & Advocate Printed at this place for a full statement of the ord[i]n[ations] sermon[s] &c of the dedication of the house of the Lord. Published in the March No. [p. 84] commencing on page 74 and ending on page 283 inclusive.[1]

NOTE

1. See *HC*, 2:410-28.

Chapter 19

Excommunication

CHAPTER 19

And it came to pass that E. Partridge, Isaac Morly, John Corrill, and W. W. Phelps left Kirtland to fill their mission in Mo. where they had left their families.

They arrived in Mo. in safety. But as soon as these men arrivd at home the Devil roared in this land and stired the old Jackson Co. Mob up to great anger, and the People in Clay Co. The afore mentioned brethren went in search of a place where the church could setle in peace and found a country North of Ray Co. that would answer the purpose, providing the few scaterd inhabitants that resided there were willing for the brethren to move there and enjoy their Religion and constitutional rights, as well as the Counties Round about.[1]

This move gave great uneasiness and the people of Clay Co. convened and some were determined to drive the brethren from the State others were opposed, and finnally we succeeded to get the consent of the people of Clay Co. and a majority of Ray to move into this <place> Now Caldwell Co.

Therefore [we] commenced setling this place Far West in

~~the summer of 1836. in august the first building was erected.~~ [p. 85] Some dificulties arose in the land of Kirtland and dissensions took place which is to be feared will end in the misery of some precious souls.[2]

Some dificulties have taken place in this County Caldwell but are now all setled to the satisfaction of all parties as I believe[.]

T. B. Marsh & D. W. Pattan have left for Kirtland Ohio, to fill a mission in there apostolic capacity.

In the fall of 1838 Joseph Smith Jr. [and] Sidney Rigdon came to Zion. On a visit — to prepare a place for them selves and families.

The situation of the Church both here and in Kirtland is in an unpleasant situation in consequence of the reorganization of its authorities, which was not satisfactory to all concerned. And has terminated in the expulsion of some members, as also some temporal movements have not proved satisfactory to all parties [and] has also terminated in the expulsion of <many> members,[3] ~~among whom is W. W. Phelps and myself. Therefore I close this history of the church of Latter Day Saints, Hoping that I may be for given of my faults, and my sins be bloted out and in the last day be saved in the kingdom of God notwithstanding my present situation, which I hope will soon be bettered and I find favor in the eyes of God and <All men> his saints Farewell March.~~ 1838.[4]

NOTES

1. See Stephen C. LeSueur, *The 1838 Mormon War in Missouri* (Columbia: University of Missouri Press, 1987).

2. Whitmer here refers to the collapse of the Kirtland Anti-Banking Safety Society and resulting apostasy.

3. For this tumultuous time in Mormon history, see Backman, *Heavens*, 310-29; and Marvin S. Hill, C. Keith Rooker, and Larry T. Wimmer, "The Kirtland Economy Revisited: A Market Critique of Sectarian Economics," *Brigham Young University Studies* 17 [Summer 1977]: 391-472.

4. This last was probably written about the time that the Saints in Missouri had rejected W. W. Phelps, John Whitmer, and David Whitmer as presidents of the Church in Zion and their subsequent excommunication on March 10, 1838 (see *Far West Record*, 121-25, 137-41, 145-50).

Until 1838 John Whitmer and his family continued to live among the Saints in Far West; however, his writing took on a distinctly anti-Mormon tone. After his family and a number of other "dissenters" were expelled from Far West, he kept up his history, largely by way of correspondence with people still in the church that he knew. These people have yet to be identified.

Chapter 20
War and Bloodshed

CHAPTER 20, 1837

[p. 86] In the fall of 1836, Joseph Smith Jr.[,] S. Rigdon[,] & others of the Leaders of the church at Kirtland[,] Ohio, Established a bank for the purpose of Speculation and the whole church partook of the same Spirit,[1] they were lifted up in pride, and lusted after the forbidden things of God such as covetousness, & in secret combination, Spiritual wife doctrine, that is pleurality of wives,[2] and gadianton bands in which they were bound. with oaths[3] &c. that brought divisins and mistrust among those who were pure in heart, and desired the upbilding of the Kingdom of God—

J. Smith Jr. & S. Rigdon & Hyrum Smith moved their families to this place Far West in the Spring of 1838. As soon as they came here they began to enforce their new organized plan in force which caused disensions and difficulties, threatnings and even murders[.] Smith Called a counsel of council he Stated that any person who said a word against the heads of the church should be driven over these prairies as a chaced deer by a pack of hounds, having an allusian to the gideonots [Gideonites] as they were then termed to Justify themselves, in their wicked designes[4] Thus on the 19th of June 1838 they preached a sermon called the Salt sermon[5] in which these gideonites understood that they should drive the disenters as they termed those who believed ~~the~~ not [p. 87] in their secret bands in fornication adultery or midnight machinations.[6] Therefore they commenced suing at the law of the land by attachment for debts which they knew were paid and Justly paid, according to the laws of God and ~~land~~ the Land & thus foreswore themselves in these things J. Smith S Rigdon & Hiram Smith were the instigators & G. W. Robinson was the prosecutor—against David Whitmer, L. E. Johnson, O. Cowdery, F. G. Williams W. W. Phelps and myself—they had threatend us to kill us if we did not make restitution to them by upholding them in their wicked purposes and designs after they had instituted the foregoing suits[.] O. Cowdery D Whitmer L. E. Johnson & myself went to Clay Co. to obtain legal counsel to prepare to over throw these attachments which they had caused to [be] sued against us which we were abundantly able to do by good and substantial witnesses

But to our great astonishment when we were on our way home from Liberty Clay Co. we met the families of O. Cowdery & L. E. Johnson whom they had driven from their homes and robed them of all their goods save clothing & bedding &c.

While we were gone Jo. & Rigdon & the band of gadeantons [Gadiantons] kept up a guard and watched our houses and abused our families and threatened them [that] if they were not gone by morning they would be drove out & threatened our lives if they ever saw us in Far West.[7]

[p. 88] After they had driven us and our families they commenced a difficulty in Davies Co. adjoining this Co. in the which they began to rob and burn houses &c &c. took honey which they (the Mormons) called Sweet oil & hogs which they called bear, and Cattle which they called Buffalo. thus they would Justify themselves by saying we are the people of God and all things are Gods, therefore they are ours, the old inhabitants were not slack in paying them in their own coin[.] Thus war and bloodshed commenced and the result was that the Church was driven from this land & the pure in heart and innocent as well as the more wicked Save a few dissenters who were left here to fulfil some of the former commandments.[8]

Now before the Church left J. Smith Jr.[,] S. Rigdon[,] H. Smith[,] P. P. Pratt[,] Lyman Wight[,] & Amasa Lyman were delivered up to Gen. [Samuel D.] Lucas & General [John B.] Clark & the rest of the officers of Government which were ordered out by the governor of this State to stop the difficulties between the citizens & Mormons—Smith & those others were tried by those officers for treason &c. but found that they were not legally authorized to execute them[.] after having found them guilty of many breaches of the law of the Land, they put them into the hand of Sivel officers of the government to be tried by <the> Law of the land.

[p. 89] And were commited to Jail but before the trial came on which was moved to some [other] of the Co[unties]. of this State where the people were not so much prej[u]diced against them, as they were moved from Clay Co. to the County where they were to be tried, they hirred the guard to let them go, &c. which they did and informed their brethren that an anger [angel] had delivered them from the guard, when in fact money hired those base & corrupt men, who let them go, and this through the wickedness of those to whom their safe keeping was committed, these men escaped the Justice of the law of the land which they had transgressed, and went unpunished at this time.[9]

NOTES

1. Most of this dissatisfaction and apostasy over "temporal affairs" came as a result of the failure of the Kirtland Safety Society Bank in the Panic of 1837 (see Backman, *Heavens*, 310-29; Max H. Parkin, "Conflict at Kirtland: A Study of the Nature and Causes of External and Internal Conflict of the Mormons in Ohio Between 1830 and 1838," M.A. thesis, Brigham Young University, 1966, 213-25; D. Paul Sampson and Larry T. Wimmer, "The Kirtland Safety Society: The Stock Ledger Book and the Bank Failure," *Brigham Young University Studies* 12 [Summer 1972]: 427-36; Scott H. Partridge, "The Failure of the Kirtland Safety Society," *Brigham Young University Studies* 12 [Summer 1972]: 437-54. The most important studies are Marvin S. Hill, C. Keith Rooker, and Larry T. Wimmer, "The Kirtland Economy Revisited: A Market Critique of Sectarian Economics," *Brigham Young University Studies* 17 [Summer 1977]: 391-472; and Dale W. Adams, "Chartering the Kirtland Bank," *Brigham Young University Studies* 23 [Fall 1983]:467-482).

2. For an overview and analysis of polygamy during this early period, see Parkin, "Conflict at Kirtland," 162-74; and Danel Bachman, "A Study of the Mormon Practice of Plural Marriage before the Death of Joseph Smith," M.A. thesis, Purdue University, 1975, 50-77. For a general history of Mormon plural marriage, see Richard S. Van Wagoner, *Mormon Polygamy: A History* (Salt Lake City: Signature Books, 1986).

3. This refers to the Danite Band, also known as the Daughters of Zion or the "Big Fan." Their activities have been the subject of some debate. Apparently, they were originally organized for the Saints' self-defense in Missouri but became more aggressive and began offensive operations as time went on (see, most importantly, Leland H. Gentry, "The Danite Band of 1838," *Brigham Young University Studies* 14 [Summer 1974]: 421-50, and "A History of the Latter-day Saints in Northern Missouri, from 1836-1839," Ph.D. diss., Brigham Young

University, 1965; as well as Dean C. Jessee and David J. Whittaker, eds., "The Last Months of Mormonism in Missouri: The Albert Perry Rockwood Journal," *Brigham Young University Studies* 28 [Winter 1988]: 5-41; Harold Schindler, *Orrin Porter Rockwell: Man of God, Son of Thunder*, 2d. rev. ed. [Salt Lake City: University of Utah Press, 1983], 28-43; and Reed C. Durham, Jr., "The Election Day Battle at Gallatin," *Brigham Young University Studies* 13 [Autumn 1972]: 36-61. Less valuable and contradictory in places is Stephen C. LeSueur, *The 1838 Mormon War in Missouri* [Columbia: University of Missouri Press, 1987], 38-53).

4. No conference minutes from this period contain such a statement, nor is such a comment to be found in the *History of the Church* or in any contemporary diary. A question also arises as to Whitmer's source for this comment: he had been excommunicated by this time and probably did not attend the meeting himself; the identity of his informant is unknown.

5. See n. 7 below.

6. The date of the "Salt Sermon" was actually July 17, 1838; unfortunately, no copy of it exists in complete form. See, however, F. Mark McKiernan, *The Voice of One Crying in the Wilderness: Sidney Rigdon, Religious Reformer* (Lawrence, KS: Coronado Press, 1971); Daryl Chase, "Sidney Rigdon, Early Mormon," M.A. thesis, University of Chicago, 1931; and LeSueur, *1838 Mormon War*, 38-40.

7. The reaction of members of the church—the development of a "fortress mentality" and the subsequent persecution of dissenters—has yet to be thoroughly studied. However, in one account Reed Peck writes:

> ... the Sunday following (June 17th) in the presense of a large congregation, S. Rigdon took his text from the fifth chapter of Mathew "Ye are the Salt of the Earth but if the salt have lost his savour wherewith shall it be salted, it is henceforth good for nothing but to be cast out and be trodden underfoot of men" From this

Scripture he undertook to prove that when men embrace the gospel and afterwards lose their faith it is the duty of the Saints to trample them under their feet[.] He informed the people that they had a set of men among them that had dissented from the church and were doing all in their power to destroy the presidency laying plans to take their lives &c., accused them of counterfeiting[,] lying[,] cheating[,] and numerous other crimes and called on the people to rise en masse and rid the county of Such a nuisance[.] He said it is the duty of this people to trample them into the earth, and if the county cannot be freed from them any other way I will assit to trample them down or to erect a gallows on the Square of Far West and hand them up as they did the gamblers at Vicksburgh and it would be an act at which the angels would smile with approbation[.]

Joseph Smith in a Short speech Sanctioned what had been Said by Rigdon though said he I don't want the brethren to act unlawfully but will tell them one thing Judas was a traitor and instead of hanging himself was hung by Peter, and with this hint the subject was dropped for the day having created a great excitement and prepared the people to execute anything that should be proposed.

On the next Tuesday these dissenters as they were termed were informed that preparations were being made to hang them up and if they did not escape their lives would be taken before night, and perceiving the rage of their enemies they fled to Ray County leaving their families and property in the hands of the Mormons[.] The wrath of the presidency and the threats of han[g]ing &c. were undoubtedly a farce acted to frighten these men from the county that they could not be spies upon their conduct or that they might deprive them of their property and indeed the proceedings of the presidency and others engaged in this affair fully justify the latter conclusion, for knowing the probable result, Geo W. Robinson Son in law of S. Rigdon had prior to their flight sworn out writs of attachment against these men by which he took possession of all their personal property, clothing & furniture, much of which was valuable and no doubt *very desirable* leaving their families to follow to Ray County almost destitute—That the claims by which this property was taken from these men were unjust and perhaps without foundation cannot be doubted by any unprejudiced person acquainted with all parties and circumstances and no testimony has ever been adduced to show that the men were ever guilty of a crime in Caldwell County[.]

These unlawful and tyrannical measures met with the censure of John Corrill[,] W. W. Phelps, John Clemenson[,] myself[,] and a few others but we were soon made sensible that we had excited suspicion, and perhaps endangered ourselves by venturing to speak unfavourably of these transations[.]

We found that the events of a few days had placed Caldwell County under a despotic government where even liberty of speech was denied to those not willing to unite in support of the new order (Reed Peck manuscript, 8-10, photocopy, Archives and Manuscripts, Harold B. Lee Library, Brigham Young University, Provo, Utah; original manuscript in Huntington Library, San Marino, California; see also LeSueur, *1838 Mormon War*, 37-40, 72-76, 131-32, 219-23).

8. A good analysis of the Mormon experience in Missouri has yet to be written. Some of the works currently available include T. Edgar Lyon, "Independence, Missouri, and the Mormons, 1827-1833," *Brigham Young University Studies* 13 (Autumn 1972): 10-19; Richard L. Bushman, "Mormon Persecutions in Missouri, 1833," *Brigham Young University Studies* 3 (Autumn 1960): 11-20; Richard L. Anderson, "New Data for Revising the Missouri 'Documentary History,'" *Brigham Young University Studies* 14 (Summer 1974): 488-501; Alma R. Blair, "The Haun's Mill Massacre," *Brigham Young University Studies* 13 (Autumn 1972): 62-67; B. H. Roberts, *A Comprehensive History of the Church of Jesus Christ of Latter-day Saints, Century I*, 6 vols. (Provo, UT: Brigham Young University Press, 1965), I:314-559; *Far West Record*; Pratt, *Autobiography*, 35-252; James B. Allen and Glen M. Leonard, *The Story of the Latter-day Saints*, 2d. rev. ed. [Salt Lake City: Deseret Book Co., 1992], 69-74, 83-88, 92-103, 113-17, 129-145; Leland H. Gentry, "A History of the Latter-day Saints in Northern Missouri from 1836-1839," Ph.D. diss., Brigham Young University, 1965; Warren A. Jennings, "Zion is Fled: The Expulsion of the Mormons from Jackson County, Missouri," Ph.D. diss., University of Florida, 1962; Max H. Parkin, "A History of the Latter-day Saints in Clay County, Missouri, from 1833 to 1837," Ph.D. diss., Brigham Young University, 1976; and, most recently, and perhaps most importantly, Clark V.

Johnson, ed., *Mormon Redress Petitions: Documents of the 1833-1838 Missouri Conflict* (Provo, UT: Religious Studies Center, 1992). Also useful is LeSueur, *1838 Mormon War*, which emphasizes—unlike earlier works—the persecution of dissenters by Mormons, a theme largely overlooked until now.

9. The rumor that the guards were bribed to release Joseph Smith and the rest of the company from prison was common at the time; however, there is no evidence to support it. See *HC*, 3:200-330; Leonard J. Arrington, "Church Leaders in Liberty Jail," *Brigham Young University Studies* 13 (Autumn 1972): 20-26; and Dean C. Jessee, "'Walls, Grates, and Screeking Iron Doors': The Prison Experience of Mormon Leaders in Missouri, 1838-1839," in *New Views of Mormon History: Essays in Honor of Leonard J. Arrington*, eds. Davis Bitton and Maureen Ursenbach Beecher (Salt Lake City: University of Utah Press, 1987), 19-42.

Chapter 21

Nauvoo

CHAPTER 21. FEB. 184-

Now after Smith &-Rigdon & those who were with him were let go they speedily went to Ill. to a place which Smith named Nauvoo, where they built a city which they called Nauvoo and began to build up a broken and scattered people—sending forth many Elders and priests &c. to proclaim to the Nations of the earth the sufferings of the Saints & also the gospel in great haste, and many received the gospel and gathered to Nauvoo and built a City—Smith received a Commandment to build a house unto the Name of the Lord, Which they speedily commenced but did not complete it before the wicked rose up and murdered Joseph & Hiram Smith.[1] Now the Mormons [(]the <as> they are called by those who do not believe in the book of Mormon) found great favor in the eyes of the Gov. and Congress of Ill. So that the Mormons had a [p. 90] charter granted for the City of Nauvoo. in which they organized themselves according to their own desires—Now according to the best information I could get[2] they the leaders protested [a]gainst Spiritual wife System & gadianton bands & their

191

wickedness publickly but I will show hereafter that they did not do as did the *Lamanites*, in the days of the Nephites when they were convinced of the incorrect traditions of their fathers for when they were once converted they remained so unto the day of their death.

As soon as the Lord gave Smith & the church favor in the eyes of the people among whom they lived, and began to prosper them and many began to gather to Nauvoo—Smith and the leaders began to excercise their hatred to those whom he called his enemies—he hired a man by the name of Porter Orin Rockwell (who was one of the gadianton band of whom I heretofore spoke of) to go and murder a man by the Name of L. W. Boggs who had been elected Gov. by the people of the state of Mo. but was not gov. at the time Smith sent him to commit this crime—Boggs Resided at Independence, the place appointed for the land of <Zion> yea the New Jerusalem. So Rockwell went to Independence and at night he went to the house of Boggs and shot him through the window but he did not kill him only wounded him severely but he recovered. Rockwell was caught and put to jail and I believe he was tried by a Jury of inquiry but [there] was not sufficient testimony to condemn him, though it is a well known fact that [p. 91] he was hired by Smith to kill Boggs[3]—Now the foregoing I have given to show that this secret band did still exist among the leaders of the church. even in Smith the Prophet & Seer & Revelator[.] had it not been upheld by him the church would not have suffered in the way it did for example look at the children of Israel in the days of King Saul[.] for his transgression the Kingdom was wrent from him, and given to another more worthy. and the Children of Israel suffered much in consequence thereof.

Now as I said before the Lord began to prosper them in

Nauvoo, and as soon as they began to prosper they began to be lifted up in pride and behaved vilely towards the people in Hancock County Illinois in which Co. Nauvoo was Situated as also to the people in the Counties round about. So that the people began to threaten them again and raised mobs to drive the Saints, (as they called themselves,) from their homes. The Mormons at the same time would steal for some came to Mo. and stole some horses, and we heard much complaint from people of Ill. for the Mormons would steal from them many things, and indeed the Mormons would Justify themselves in this wickedness by saying We are the Lords, and the earth is the Lords, & the fullness thereof. therefore these things are ours. also, God has said by the mouths of the Prophets that he would consecrate the riches of the Gentiles to the House of Israel and we are the House of Israel &c. &. Now say they when these things are placed before our eyes go [p. 92] God is not intending to give it himself but you are agents, and these things are before you go and help yourselves &c.

Now these Scriptures would they quote to excuse themselves that they might steal and Rob their Neighbors according to their wicked desires lusting after those things which were forbidden them in the Scriptures.

After the Mormons had their city Chartered by the state Legislature they had all their officers, and when any Stole, they would flee to Nauvoo. to seek protection, and. behold they were protected and upheld so that the guilty could not be punished according to the Law of the land. Now had the Leaders been willing to bring the guilty to Justice they could not have escaped but must have been punished, but here is the bad affect of Secret combinations such as have ever destroyed the church of God because those who were leaders in the church were partakers of these Cain institutions which were handed down by the devil.[4]—

In the mean while the Twelve were Preaching in England[5] and else where and built up many churches the gathering continued, and many who were born again and came to Nauvoo and beheld the things that were there conducted, sickened in their hearts, others were pleased with those things for they were pleasing to the carnal mind, especially when an assurance was held forth for their protection by the [p. 93] Prophet of God. Others dined [denied] the faith for they knew that these things were contrary to the word of God and withdrew themselves.[6]

Now there has been much said <and published> by the mobbers of Illinois & Mo. that are without a shadow of truth as also by the people of Nauvoo.

Now Smith wrote many Revelations concerning himself as you will see by Reading the book of Covenants Printed at Kirtland[,] Ohio[,] in which we read that the Keys of the Kingdom, should not be taken from him until Christ should come, on conditions that he should not transgress. But if he should transgress they should be taken and another be appointed in his stead, and that this should be all the power that he should have to appoint another in his stead.[7]

~~God knowing all things prepared a man whom he visited by an angel of God and showed him where there were some ancient Record hid, and also put in his heart to desire of Smith to Grant him power to establish a stake to Zion in Wisconsin Territory, whose name is James J. Strang. Now at first Smith was unfavorably disposed to grant him this request, but being troublied in spirit and knowing from the things that were staring him in his face that his days must soon be closed therefore he enquired of the of the Lord and behold the Lord said, Appoint~~ [p. 94] ~~James J. Strang the Prophet Seer <&> Revelator unto my church for thou shalt thereby do a mission,~~

~~thy~~ [Wife] ~~is [better] &c. Shortly after this appointment of Strang, the mob gathered and took by Strategem~~ Joseph & Hyrum Smith ~~conveyed them to~~ Carthage the Seat of Justice ~~in & for the Co. of Caldwell.~~ <Hancock> ~~as if to~~ try them ~~by the law of the land but instead of trying them by the law of the land for their crimes,~~ they murdered them, ~~& thus the Lords annointed fell by the brutal hand of man, & they are gone the way of all the earth, and~~ [James] ~~Strangs Reigns in the place of Smith the author and proprietor of the Book of Mormon.~~[8]

As I have before stated that Joseph Smith had left Kirtland[,] Ohio[,] with the Camp of the Saints so called, to go to Jackson Co. to redeem Zion and received a Revelation that God would redeem it in his own time &c. On his way to Mo. or Zion he was frequently heard to say that he had a duty to perform and that was [that] he had to appoint another in his stead to Wit David Whitmer.

After the Camp was dispersed at fishing River Smith & F. G. Williams came to Clay County together with many others who Scatterd in Clay Co & elsewhere Smith called a conference at the house of Lyman Wight three miles West of Liberty, in which Confranc the most of the official number belonging in Zion were present, Where Smith organized the [p. 95] High Council of Zion as I said in a former chapter in which David Whitmer was ordained President of Zion & John Whitmer & W. W. Phelps his counsellors. Here at the same time he ordained David Whitmer Prophet Seer Revelator & translator.[9]

NOTES

1. See James B. Allen and Glen M. Leonard, *The Story of the Latter-day Saints*, 2d. rev. ed. (Salt Lake City: Deseret Book Co., 1992), 153-228.

2. Note that Whitmer admits he was not present for the events he is discussing: he is relying on "the best information I could get."

3. See Harold Schindler, *Orrin Porter Rockwell: Man of God, Son of Thunder*, 2d. rev. ed. (Salt Lake City: University of Utah Press, 1983), 67-73. Although Rockwell was charged with the crime, such allegations against him, or charges that Joseph Smith hired him to assassinate Boggs, have never been proven.

4. See Kenneth W. Godfrey, "Causes of Mormon Non-Mormon Conflict in Hancock County, Illinois, 1839-1846," Ph.D. diss., Brigham Young University, 1967.

5. For an overview of the missionary work of the Twelve Apostles conducted in England during this period (1839-41), see James B. Allen, Ronald K. Esplin, and David J. Whittaker, *Men with a Mission: The Quorum of the Twelve Apostles in the British Isles, 1837-1841* (Salt Lake City: Deseret Book Co., 1992), 67-322.

6. The extent of apostasy among new converts for these reasons is not known.

7. D&C 43:1-4; see Wood, 2[1835]:125-26. For background, see Cook, *Revelations*, 61-62, 132.

8. After Joseph and Hyrum were killed, Whitmer's initial sympathies were with the leadership claims made by charismatic Mormon dissident James J. Strang. The exact extent of Whitmer's activities with the group, however, is unknown; it would seem, though, from the writing of his history, that his belief in that group was a short one (see Steven L. Shields, *Divergent Paths of the Restoration* 4th rev. ed. [Los Angeles, CA: Restoration Research, 1990], 40-46; and Roger Van Noord, *King of Beaver Island: The Life and Assassination of James Jesse Strang* [Urbana: University of Illinois Press, 1988].)

9. Concerning this incident, David Whitmer wrote:

To show you that Brother Joseph and myself still loved each other as brethren after this, I will tell you that he had so much confidence in me in July, 1834, he ordained me his successor as "Prophet Seer and Revelator" to the Church. He did this of his own free will and not at any solicitation whatsoever on my part. I did not know what he was going to do until he laid his hands upon me and ordained me.

... I supposed this is news to many of you—that Brother Joseph ordained me his successor—but it is in your records, and there are men now living who were present in that council of elders when he did it, in the camp of Zion, on Fishing River, Missouri, July 1834 (*An Address to All Believers in Christ, by a Witness to the Divine Authenticity of the Book of Mormon* [Richmond, MO: David Whitmer, 1887], 55; photocopy, Special Collections, Harold B. Lee Library, Brigham Young University, Provo, Utah; more importantly, see *Far West Record*, 151-52).

Chapter 22

Dispersion

CHAPTER 22ND

Now from this time forth which was in July 1834 Smith seemed to be in doubt where unto this thing would grow and began to upbraid D. Whitmer and abuse him as his natural custom was to do with those whom he feared, least they should become great in the sight of God or man, therefore, he haranged the conference and sought to destroy the confidence of the people present in D. Whitmer on whom he had bestowed all the gifts & power that he had himself received by inspiration by the laying on his hand according to the order of Heaven.

After Smiths return to Kirtland[,] Ohio[,] and after his ordering the first Elders of the church to go to Ohio there to receive their endowment from on high he hasted the finishing of the house at Kirtland which was commenced before he had gone to Zion to redeem her. He from this time began to be lifted up in the pride of his eyes, and began to seek riches and the glory of the world, also sought to establish the ancient order of things, as he & his counsellors Rigdon & Hyrum Smith pleased to call it. Therefore they began to [p. 96] form themselves into a secret Society which they termed the Brother of Gideon, in the which Society they took oaths that they would support a brother wright or wrong even to the sheding of blood.

thus those who belonged [to] this society were bound to Keep it a profound Secret never to reveal but ever to conceal these abominations from all and every person axcept those who were of the same Craft. But these things could not be kept a secret in consequence of betreyers who fel from their faith and revealed their Secrets.

thus things were carried on by Secret plots and midnight machinations, which Society was beginning to be established in Kirtland[,] Ohio[,] in the fall of 1836.[1]

The formation of these things together with adultery wickedness and abominations which grew and Multiplied in the heads and members of the Church of Christ of Latter Day Saints Brought Joseph Smith & his brother Hiram to an untimely end and also the scattering of the Church and [the] twelve who assumed the authority of leading the Church were Scattered from Nauvoo and Suffered great Affliction. As also James J. Strang who also professes to be appointed by a letter received from Joseph as being appointed Seer Revelator Profit & Successor of him Joseph, also Sidney Rigdon he drew away a portion after him.[2]

Now it came to pass that the twelve of whom Brigham Young is leader is [manuscript ends]

NOTES

1. Whitmer is probably the only historian who has dated the origin of the Danite band (what he here terms Brother of Gideon) to 1836 in Kirtland; no other source yet known confirms this. In addition, this statement contradicts his earlier one

which stated that the Danites were organized in Missouri two years later, following Sidney Ridgon's "Salt Sermon." In the statement concerning Kirtland, Whitmer blames the band's origins on Joseph Smith and the rest of the First Presidency of the church. It would be interesting to know what evidence he had of the Kirtland origins of the movement, if any. *Answers to this are provided in Quinn - Origins of Power*

2. Strang and Rigdon—both of whom have been discussed in earlier notes—were only two of a number of people who tried to assume the leadership of the church after the prophet's death. Among this number were William Smith, Lyman Wight, William Bickerton, and John E. Page, as well as Brigham Young and the Quorum of the Twelve (see D. Michael Quinn, "The Mormon Succession Crisis of 1844," *Brigham Young University Studies* 16 [Winter 1976]: 187-233).

INDEX

A

Abbott, Lewis, 140
Albany, New York, 102-103
Aldrich, Hazen, 141
Allen, Charles, 106
Apostasy, 69, 81-82, 85, 87, 180
Apostates, 183-85
Apostles, 140-41, 194
Atchison, David R., 108

B

Baldwin, Wheeler, 87
Barnsley Independent Church, 165-67
Bebee, Calvin, 135-37, 140
Bebee, Isaiah, 140
Bible, 41, 101
Billings, Titus, 140
Boggs, Lilburn W., 192
Book of Enoch, 7
Book of Mormon, 56
Booth, Ezra, 70, 86
Boston, Massachusetts, 102-103
Bowers, William, 107
Boynton, John F., 140-41
Brace, Truman, 140
Brackenberry, Joseph, 87
Braziale, Hugh L., 108
Burke, J. M., 140

Burnett, Serenes, 101

C

Cahoon, Reynolds, 70, 139
Caldwell County, 179, 180
Campbell, Mr., 106
Campbell, Samuel, 131-32
Carter, Jared, 140
Carter, Simeon, 135-37, 140
Chapin, Adolphus, 140
Chardon, Ohio, Branch, 82-83
Childs, Henry, 108
Cholera, 132
Church government, 140-42, 167-70
Clark, General John B., 185
Clay County, 179, 185
Coe, Joseph, 86, 140
Colesville, New York, Branch, 7, 12-13, 86
Coltrin, Zebedee, 140, 141
Conferences, 8-9, 41, 69-71, 85, 98, 101, 195
Consecration, law of, 27-34, 37
Copley, Leman, 57, 81-83
Corrill, John, 71, 87, 106, 111-12, 119-21, 121-23, 126-27, 129, 135-37, 139, 173, 179
Cowdery, Oliver, 3, 13, 55-56, 85-87, 101, 102, 139, 142,

170, 173, 174, 184
Cummings, Mr., 106

D

Daniels, Solomon, 140
Danites, 183-85, 191-93, 199-200
Daviess County, 184-85
Death, 42
Demillo, Freeborn, 140
Dibble, Philo, 140
Doniphan, Alexander, 108
Dunklin, Daniel, 112-13, 121-23, 126-27, 127-28, 135-37
Durphey, Edmund, 140

E

Elders, 167-70
Endowment, 137, 174-75, 199-200

F

False spirits, 37-38, 57-58, 71
Far West, 179-80, 183-85
First Presidency, 167-70
Franklin, Lewis, 106
Fristoe, Judge, 106

G

Gause, Jesse, 102
Gilbert, Algernon Sidney, 106, 111-12, 119-21, 121-23, 126-27, 128-29
Grant, A. C., 140
Graves, E. H., 174

Gregg, Harmon, 108

H

Hancock, Levi, 140, 141
Hancock, Solomon, 140
Hancock County, 193
Harris, Emer, 87
Harris, John, 108
Harris, Martin, 56, 70, 86, 139, 142
Healings, 42, 56-57, 87
Hebrew school, 174
Hewett, John, 165-67
Hicks, Russell, 106
Higbee, Elias, 174
High council, 135, 174, 195
High priesthood, 69-71
High priests, 167-70
Hinkle, George M., 174
Hitchcock, Jesse, 140, 174
Hubble, 37-38
Hyde, Orson, 140, 141

I

Irvin, W. L., 108

J

Jackson, Andrew, 113-19, 119-21
Jackson County, 102, 103-105, 106, 108, 111-24, 125, 179
Johnson, John, 140
Johnson, Luke, 140-41
Johnson, Lyman E., 140-41, 184
Joseph of Egypt, 167
Judgments, 42

K

Kimball, Heber C., 140-41
Kirtland, Ohio, 3, 12-13, 13-14, 27, 37-41, 42, 51-52, 69-71, 85, 137, 179, 180, 199-200
Kirtland Bank (Kirtland Anti-Banking Safety Society), 183
Kirtland temple, 177
Knight, Joseph, Jr., 140
Knight, Newell, 81-82, 86, 135-37, 140

L

Lewis, Joshua, 140
Liberty, Missouri, 195
Lucas, Judge, 106
Lucas, Samuel D., 128, 129, 185
Lyman, Amasa, 185

M

Miracles, 56-57
Missionaries, 3, 42, 47, 55, 56-57, 81, 87, 98-99, 101, 191
Missouri, 82, 82-83, 85, 85-87, 88-91, 98-99, 101, 102, 103-106, 106-108, 111-23, 167-170, 179, 180
Morley, Isaac, 70, 71, 87, 106, 135-37, 139, 179
Mummies, 167
Murdock, John, 47, 70, 87, 140

N

Nauvoo, Illinois, 191-95
Nauvoo temple, 191
New Jerusalem, 51-52
New York, 51-52, 56-57, 69, 71, 102-103
New York City, New York, 98-99
Non-believers, 47-48

O

Oldham, Leonidas, 107
Olmstead, N. K., 107
Overton, Aaron, 108
Owens, Samuel C., 107

P

Page, Hiram, 56, 140
Partridge, Edward, 4, 37, 70-71, 87, 106, 108, 111-12, 119-21, 121-23, 126-27, 129, 157-37, 139, 179
Patten, David W., 140-41, 180
Peck, Ezekiel, 140
Peck, Hezekiah, 140, 170
Persecutions, 42, 47, 85, 103-105, 106-108, 179-80
Peterson, Ziba, 3
Petitions, 111-24
Pettigrew, David, 140
Phelps, Waterman, 137
Phelps, William W., 86, 106, 108, 111-12, 119-21, 121-23, 126-27, 127-28, 128-29, 135-37, 139, 170, 173, 174, 179, 180, 184, 195
Pitkin, George, 140
Polygamy, 183, 191-92
Pratt, Orson, 56-57, 140-41, 174
Pratt, Parley P., 3, 70, 87, 135-

37, 140-41, 174, 185
Prophecies, 69-71, 173-74
Pryor, Abel, 140

R

Ray County, Missouri, 179
Reese, Amos, 108
Revelations, 5-7, 7-8, 9-12, 13, 27-34, 37-41, 42, 47-48, 51-52, 55-56, 57-58, 81-83, 98, 173, 194
Rich, Leonard, 141
Rigdon, Sidney, 3-4, 4-5, 5-7, 8, 27, 70, 86, 88-91, 101, 102, 139, 170, 173, 174, 180, 183-84, 185, 199-200
Robinson, G. W., 184
Rockwell, Orrin Porter, 192
Ryland, John S., 111-12

S

Salt Sermon, 184
Seixas, Joshua, 174
Seventies, 141-42
Shakers (United Society of Believers in Christ's Second Coming), 57
Shaw, Thomas, 165-66
Sherman, Lyman, 141
Simpson, G. W., 106-107
Smith, Don Carlos, 139
Smith, Hyrum, 56, 70, 139, 173, 174, 183-85, 191, 199-200
Smith, John, 140
Smith, Joseph, Jr., 4, 5-7, 8-9, 9-12, 13-14, 27-34, 41, 55-56, 69-71, 81-83, 85-87, 101, 102-103, 131-33, 135, 137, 139, 167, 170, 173-74, 180, 183-84, 185, 191-95, 199-200
Smith, Joseph, Sr., 56, 139
Smith, Samuel H., 56-57, 139
Smith, Sylvester, 141
Smith, William, 139
Spiritual gifts, 103
Stanton, Daniel, 140
Strang, James J., 194-95, 200

T

Temples, 85-87, 191
Thayer, Ezra, 70
Thompson, Ohio, Branch, 81-82, 82-83
Tippetts, Captain, 106

W

Wakefield, Joseph, 70
Waller, Z., 107
Weston, Samuel, 108
Whitlock, Harvey, 70
Whitmer, Christian, 56, 139
Whitmer, David, 56, 108, 135-37, 139, 142, 173, 174, 184, 195, 199
Whitmer, Jacob, 56, 140
Whitmer, John, 3, 13, 55-56, 102, 106, 111-12, 119-21, 121-23, 126-27, 129, 135-37, 139, 170, 173, 174, 180, 184, 195
Whitmer, Peter, Jr., 3, 56, 86, 139

Whitmer, Peter, Sr., 139
Whitney, Newell K., 88, 101, 102-103, 139
Wight, Lyman, 55, 70, 135-37, 140, 185, 195
Williams, Frederick G., 139, 170, 173, 174, 184, 195
Wilson, Mr., 106

Y

Young, Brigham, 140-41, 200
Young, Joseph, 141
Younger, Harvey H., 108

Z

Zion's Camp, 131-33, 195